# Plays Without People

# Plays Without People

PUPPETRY AND SERIOUS DRAMA

## Peter D. Arnott

———————— ✳ ————————

WITH AN INTRODUCTION BY

### Hubert C. Heffner

————

Indiana University Press · Bloomington

PICTURE CREDITS

Plates 1 and 2 are reproduced by courtesy of the University of Iowa News and Information Service; plates 3-8 and 21-25 are by Michael Gillette; plates 9-20 are by Orazio Fumagalli.

FOR CHRISTOPHER GRANT

# CONTENTS

# LIST OF PLATES

# FOREWORD

SOME YEARS AGO when H. D. F. Kitto, that masterly interpreter of Greek tragedy, was visiting with us at Indiana University, he told me of a remarkable experience which he had
recently had in witnessing a performance of Euripides' *Medea*
done with puppets. He said when he first heard that a young
teacher of Greek, then serving in one of the colleges in Wales,
was performing Greek tragedy in this manner, he assumed
that such a representation would be ludicrous; hence when he
later had an opportunity to see the *Medea*, he went out of
curiosity prepared to be quietly amused. To his amazement,
when the play was over, he realized that he had forgotten all
about puppets and amusement and had witnessed a remarkably moving performance of Euripides' tragedy. The young
man who did that performance, Peter Arnott, said Kitto, had
not only brought the ancient play to life, but had done so in
a remarkably fluid and effective translation.

Several years thereafter Peter Arnott crossed the Atlantic
to join the faculty of the State University of Iowa in the Department of Classics, with connections also in the Department
of Speech and Dramatic Art. We invited him to come to
Indiana University to perform the *Medea*, and later other
plays, for our students and faculty. Those performances
have amply shown me that Kitto's praise was by no means
overpraise. His evocation of the spirit of the play with his
puppet characters, be that play *Medea*, *Everyman*, *Doctor
Faustus*, or any other in his repertory, is remarkably faithful

to the play's affective meaning. Several years ago I had the pleasure of seeing, in the University Theatre at the State University of Iowa, Peter Arnott's production with live actors of his translation of Aristophanes' *The Frogs*. I have seen only one other production of Greek comedy brought to life on the stage that could compare with Arnott's. That was a performance of *The Birds* staged at Catholic University in Washington, D.C., by Walter Kerr. The production of *The Frogs* was an amazing performance. Until I saw it, I would never have dreamed that this somewhat esoteric ancient comedy could be so brought to life for a modern American audience. It literally had everything. So much so that after the play was over I said to Professor Arnott, in congratulating him, that I was glad that a classicist had done the production. He immediately asked, "Do you think it was unfaithful to Aristophanes?" I think the dramatist himself, had Dionysus brought him back, would have heartily approved the revival. Certainly the audience did.

I mention these personal experiences in order to vouch for Peter Arnott's mastery, not merely of puppetry, but of the art of stage interpretation of drama, especially drama of the past. His successes illustrate the crucial necessity of a thorough understanding and mastery of the dramatic text for the effective recreation of drama upon the stage. No one would deny or minimize the importance of a thorough comprehension of, and skills in, the techniques and methods of theatre arts for the actor, the director, the designer, and the technician. Even a hasty reading of *Plays Without People* will reveal that such a denial is foreign to Arnott's point of view. But techniques are not enough; their mastery can at best result in merely highly-trained technicians dependent upon men of understanding. Technique without understanding can lead to mere stage trickery, sometimes evident in American university theatre productions of plays from the past. Techniques have no validity in themselves. They are merely means to an end, a means to an adequate interpretation of a specific play, upon a specific stage, for a specific audience. Stage and audience are important, yes; but a full comprehension of the play in all of its evocative powers and effects comes first.

*Plays Without People* is not, therefore, an elementary manual about the making and operation of puppets. It is about that which comes first—the play and its interpretation. The author's chief concern is to reveal the way in which he studies, analyzes, and prepares plays for presentation by his figures on his stage for different audiences, ranging from elementary school children to adult members of academic faculties. As he says, this work is "a record of something which began as an experiment and ended as a conviction, if not an obsession— the idea that puppets, or more specifically marionettes, could be used for the performance of serious drama, and could contribute something of value to the revival of plays of certain important periods."

His book, however, is much more than a record, much more than an advanced treatise for experienced puppeteers. It is a source of ideas and insights for every dedicated interpreter of drama upon the stage. For example, he illustrates repeatedly and effectively a statement which he quotes, as follows: "Art, it has been wisely said, is not addition but subtraction; what you leave out is more important than what you put in." The puppet stage, as Arnott makes crystal clear, by its very nature forces this principle of artistic simplicity upon its practition- ers. The living stage, especially in the nineteenth century and all too often in our age, has so obscured that fundamental axiom that it is all but forgotten. Modern realistic representa- tional methods are as reprehensible in this respect as were the nineteenth-century romantic "picturizing" performances. Fortunately, the very nature of the puppet denies to the pup- pet stage the realistic style; in this theatre the lesson is strik- ingly enforced, as it is not too often in the living theatre, that "art is subtraction." Throughout the book Arnott draws other striking contrasts between and comparisons with the puppet and the living stage. Thus the book is as important to the artist in the latter theatre as it is to the puppeteer. His comparisons and contrasts are often startlingly revealing, always illuminating.

In his discussion of the puppet stage as a means of reviving great plays from the past, Professor Arnott insists that certain kinds of plays are amenable to adequate interpretation by puppets, while other kinds are not. Both the kind of action which constitutes the plot and the kind of characterizations of the agents are controlling factors in determining suitability. To the extent that the action of a play depends upon a highly localized place and an exactly specified time, to that extent the action is dependent upon and is also a projection of selected but often minute details of environment. In such plays the agents are likely to be differentiated by a complex series of physical and psychological traits. Such characters are most difficult, if not impossible, to present by means of puppets, says Arnott. When the characterization requires that the inner state of the character—his sensations, feelings, emotions, passions, and suffering—must be rendered largely by the art of the actor rather than by the art of the poet-dramatist, such renderings become increasingly impossible for the puppet. For example, I have never seen a puppet performance in which a puppet wept with serious convincingness. There seems always to be an element of the ludicrous about the weeping puppet. There are great plays, however, in which both the action and the characters are highly universalized. In such plays the incidents of the action are reduced to an essential minimum and the characters are individualized with a few great, starkly presented, traits. Such artistic reduction or subtraction carried further results in characters becoming highly universalized types or even personified abstractions and the events of the action constituting an allegory. Of this latter kind is the medieval morality play *Everyman*, in Arnott's repertory. Representative of the former kind in his repertory are the Greek plays and Racine's *Phèdre*.

What Arnott has to say throughout his book on these differences constitutes a revealing commentary upon the art of acting, a potential illumination for the experienced actor and a valuable lesson to the student of acting. The discussion should serve to make the actor acutely aware of the different styles demanded by different plays and periods. He can learn even more about the utilization of style by the living actor from witnessing a puppet performance by Arnott of, say, Euripides' *Medea*. The book and the performance should serve to make him aware of how little of the art of acting is embraced in the so-called "Method."

The discussion of suitable and unsuitable plays contains revelations also for the student of drama. It serves, for example, to broaden our perspective on the nature and constrictions of the "realistic" style in both the composition and the interpretation on the stage of that kind of drama that became increasingly dominant from the eighteenth century to contemporary times. Thereby it raises by implication questions of theory. The acceptance and response of audiences to the performance of serious plays by puppets challenges the conventionally accepted and narrowly interpreted "doctrine of illusion." That doctrine, which in its modern acceptance stems from Samuel Taylor Coleridge, rests upon the ancient confusion of art and nature. Coleridge realized, but so far as I am aware never made explicitly clear, that illusion had to be understood as an exercise of the fancy and the imagination and not as absolute identification. He well understood that the human imagination was capable of various kinds of illusion; but nineteenth-century realism (we should say realisms) and naturalism interpreted the concept into an almost absolute doctrine of psychological, kinesthetic identification. That latter interpretation dominates the large body of psychological literature on the subject of empathy and has consequently

permeated modern criticism. Yet it is amply evident that two
highly effective performances of *Medea*, one by puppets and
the other by live actors, have different affective powers within themselves and hence upon audiences. These differences
need extensive examination, far more extensive than time and
space will here allow.

One of the obvious differences lies in the diverse renderings
of character possible to the two kinds of actors. Yet another
difference which stems from and extends the first is found in
the separate kind of relationship between actor and audience
of the puppet stage and the stage of living actors. Let us
look for a moment at the eponymous agent Agamemnon in
Aeschylus' tragedy. It is apparent that he is a highly ab-
stracted, though not an abstract, character. He has few traits
of character but he has all that are necessary to his function in
the plot. Since he was well and widely known to the Greeks
through the compositions of both the dramatic and non-
dramatic poets from Homer onward, his configuration in
Aeschylus' play doubtless evoked a much more complete personality than would a reading or witnessing of that play today. Imagination pieced out any imperfections in the poor
shadow of Agamemnon. In the play the relatively few indications of character are summed up in the all-encompassing and
frightfully symbolic decision at his homecoming to tread the
purple carpet into his house of doom. Since that decision represents characterization on its most highly formal level, nothing more is needed in the depiction of Agamemnon for the
ensuing action. In the play he is a gigantic monolithic figure.

On the stage the live actor will expand somewhat this monolithic representation but that expansion must be carefully
controlled, carefully styled to remain faithful to the Aeschy-
lean intent and effect. The actor's expansion inevitably occurs
because he contributes something of his own psychic personality to the role. That contribution will appear in a variety of
elements. It will appear in the tone and range of voice, as well

as in the meaning, including the implication, of each line conveyed through the oral delivery. The live actor will thus impart something of his own thought, feelings, and understanding to the character of Agamemnon. In assimilating his conception of the man Agamemnon and in attempting to project that conception he must inevitably color the character with his own essential nature. That coloring and expansion will appear not merely in vocal rendering. It will appear in the stance and posture, the repose and the movements of the body, including movements of the torso, turning of the head, and gesture. If the role is played without a mask and in a not too large theatre, it will appear notably in the use of the eyes and all of the mobile features of the face. This psychic contribution of the actor to the character will naturally change from actor to actor and will thereby vary, even if in a most subtle and imperceptible manner, the relation between actor and audience.

That relationship is far more complex than most discussions of the theory of illusion would have us believe. However effective his performance, no actor is going to delude an intelligent adult audience into believing he is actually Agamemnon, who is in very truth slaughtered by Clytemnestra. If the enactment of the role is artistically effective, there will certainly be varying degrees of identification between members of the audience and the actor. At the same time those members will realize the artistic excellence of the actor's performance as a performance and will respond to their appreciation of that artistry. Such audiences, therefore, at all theatrical performances maintain a kind of alienation, while they are also and simultaneously interacting with the actor. That very interaction constitutes a part of the actor's performance; a skilled and mature actor plays not merely a role, he plays audiences.

The audience, too, has an audience personality and a realm within which its collective imagination operates. This entity is separate and different from that of the stage occupied by the actors. Except for certain kinds of effects, it is undesirable, even dangerous, for the actor to intrude upon the identity and into the realm of the audience. An obvious example of the warranted breaking of this alienation is seen in the comedian who for the shock value steps forward out of character and comments directly to the audience about the role he is playing or an event within the play. The resultant laugh from the audience attests to the comic effectiveness of this kind of shock. The shock results from the momentary usurpation of audience identity and the consequent destruction of the separation of the two realms. The device is employed in various ways by the comic dramatist and may be legitimate in the prologues and certain types of soliloquies in serious drama. Other examples of its utilization by a dramatist may be observed in the ways in which Thornton Wilder employs the prologue-choral character in *Our Town* and the still different ways in which he requires the characters in *The Skin of Our Teeth* to cross the boundary line into the realm of the audience. These plays alone should have made amply clear the inadmissibility of a strict interpretation of the theory of illusion.

By way of a note, I hope it is sufficiently clear that I am not talking about Bertolt Brecht's so-called and often discussed "principle of *verfremdung*." In Brechtian theory that so-called principle (the word "device" would be more exact) is based upon the false assumption that the standard drama—that drama which, as he says, has an Aristotelian catharsis—must be a drama of complete illusion. In the second place, he seemingly grounds his whole conception of alienation upon his—the author's—didactic purpose. Though he produces alienation in various ways, whatever the manner of its effectuation, it is apparently designed for a single function, a function open to grave questions on artistic grounds in dramatic form. That function is apparently to present and to emphasize the playwright's own personal, private, and intruded propaganda. When the audience is composed of dedicated partisans who have come to the performance to have their convictions and opinions recharged, I presume they may derive a certain kind of satisfaction from these breaks in the action and transgression of the boundaries for the sake of a propagandistic message. I must confess that in the Brecht plays that I have seen I often found them merely annoyingly distracting. They have forced me to conclude that in writing the play Brecht was simply a dramatist *manqué*.

But that is a subject for later and more complete examination elsewhere; our concern here is a definition of some of the differences between the stage of the living actor and that of the puppet. Agamemnon is a role which, in accordance with Arnott's own ideas, could be splendidly performed by a puppet. So rendered it would create different effects and establish different audience relations from that of the living actor. We have seen that Aeschylus has created the role by a process of subtraction, so to speak. He has reduced the characterization to the minimum essential, which the performance of the living actor expands and fills out. A performance by a puppet results in a further subtraction. I suspect that Professor Arnott would say that the puppeteer speaking through the puppet adds something of that psychic personality of the performer analogous to that supplied by the living actor. Something, yes, but a very limited something. If there is a single puppeteer, his personality must be infused in and communicated through all of the characters in the play. He thereby of necessity restricts the endowment which he may confer upon any one character. The restriction is further apparent in every movement and gesture of the puppet itself. Even the relatively few potential movements allowed Agamemnon in the play must be further reduced in puppet performance. Imagine the variety and richness of meaning which the experienced actor might convey by that walk across the purple carpet. Contrast this with the stark though effective simplicity of the puppet performing that walk. The inescapable subtraction of detail results in a further abstractness of characterization. Moreover, those traits of character which are retained are given a generality by the puppet.

There is, in consequence, a different kind of relationship between audience and puppet from that which obtains between living actor and audience. The psychic distance between audience and puppet performers is considerably wider. There is really no possibility of the puppet actor responding to and utilizing audience reactions. Even though the puppeteer as the master manipulator may sense these reactions keenly, there is relatively little that he can do in making the puppet actor respond to and utilize them. Even when the puppet performance becomes so effective that the audience tends to be dominantly conscious of the actors as puppets, there still remains an extended distance between the realm of the audience and that of the actor. That alienation is requisite to the artistic interpretation of certain plays and those are the plays from which Arnott has drawn his repertory.

What is startling about Arnott's book and about his successful performances is his demonstrated contention that serious drama may be represented by means of puppets and can thereby convey to audiences a large measure of its affective powers and meanings. Serious characterization requires a degree of sympathetic understanding (but not always identification) if the characterization is to produce its proper effects. Comic characterization, by contrast, requires a measure of disassociation. With many types of comic characterization association would be detrimental to the effectiveness of the presentation and identification would prove fatal. Thus one would assume without Arnott's demonstrations that puppets might make Aristophanic comic characters highly effective but not the characters of Greek tragedy. Both his book and his performances pose the necessity for a reexamination of dramatic theory.

HUBERT C. HEFFNER

*Bloomington, Indiana*

# Plays Without People

# Introduction

This small book is a personal record of something which began as an experiment and ended as a conviction, if not an obsession—the idea that puppets, or more specifically marionettes, could be used for the performance of serious drama, and could contribute something of value to the revival of plays of certain important periods. It would be foolish and presumptuous even to hint that this is a new idea, or that my applications of it are particularly new. As I have tried to show at greater length in Chapter One, there are historical precedents for such ideas, and in many countries, though not in the United States or Great Britain, puppetry is still considered as an artistic medium of significant potential. If I can claim any originality at all, it is in the way that I have approached the medium. Although my interest in, and love for, puppets goes back to my earliest childhood, it was not for their own sake that I first began to use them seriously, but rather as an adjunct to live theatre, in an attempt to solve certain problems of play revival which still seem to me, in terms of the live theatre itself, insoluble. I have gone into these problems in more detail in Chapter Two, particularly in regard to the Greek tragic and comic drama, which remains my chief field of interest; but, for the sake of establishing a starting point, it may be helpful to state them briefly here.

On the question of reviving plays, particularly Greek plays, there are two main schools of thought. One holds that the play, ideally, should be presented in the style and setting in which it first appeared. The limitations of our knowledge are such that this is not always possible; but even so, it is argued, the director should aim at a close approximation. The other school holds that this "archaeological" approach is false and pedantic. Rather, the play should be considered in terms of the modern stage and what this has to offer. The new resources which science has put into the theatre's hands, and the results of more modern studies into the theory and nature of acting, should be exploited to their fullest extent.

It has always seemed to me that the truth lies somewhere between these two extremes, and that the process of play revival is closely akin to that of translation—is, in fact, a wider aspect of translation. The translator working from Greek, Latin, French, German, or any other language is not content merely to render the words into English—not, at any rate, if he wishes to produce something of greater value than a study aid. His task is also to render into modern terms the effect which the original work would have had on the original reader or spectator. To do this, he must have first an accurate scholarly knowledge of the language and stylistic devices that his author used; secondly, he must evaluate, in terms of the social background and artistic preconceptions of the period, the purpose that these devices served and the need to which they responded; thirdly, he must consider how best he can reproduce the effect of these devices for his own public, who have, often, a completely different set of standards and pre-conceptions. Often this means that he must depart substantially from the letter of his text. To take two notorious examples, it is generally acknowledged that the limitations of the English language make it impossible to render accurately

such rhyme-schemes as Dante's *terza rima* or Racine's Alex-
andrines. Yet they cannot be completely disregarded. The
conscientious translator will labor to find some equivalent
means of expression, more natural to the English language,
which will convey to the reader not only what the author
said but, at least approximately, the way in which he said it.

On the stage as in literature, this problem assumes its most
desperate form in works which were conceived to be presented in a highly formal and artificial way. The two most
obvious examples are Greek tragedy and French neoclassical
tragedy, itself largely modelled on the Greek. In each case the
plays were composed for a theatre whose last consideration
was the realistic representation of everyday life. In their
speech and their modes of stage behavior the characters created a world set apart from that in which their audiences
lived, and offered a performance which relied heavily on
formal movement patterns and stage conventions which the
spectators of the period understood and could interpret to
their own satisfaction. And the writing and the stage presentation were so closely integrated, and had so strong a mutual
influence, that it is impossible to consider one without the
other.

What happens in revival? It is possible, in some cases, to
achieve an almost exact reproduction of the original performance conditions, at least so far as the stage itself is concerned.
But the audience has also changed. What was meaningful to
Louis XIV and his court is meaningless to a modern audience
—except, perhaps, to an audience of scholars; but even they
have to make a conscious effort of will to put themselves back
into the period, and in the exercising of this act of will the
freedom of response is lost. This change in reaction may be
due to several causes. In the case of the Greek plays, as I shall
suggest later, it stems largely from a shift in spatial relation-
ships, in French drama from the disappearance of a once
familiar acting style. The history of the Comédie Française

demonstrates clearly the dangers of preserving a style of performance that has lost popular acceptance; it is only comparatively recently that this company has achieved a satisfactory compromise between the demands of the old plays and those of the new audience. Modern spectators, at least so far as the serious drama is concerned, are not sympathetic to formal acting or presentation. There are encouraging signs that this is an attitude which may soon change, but at present the problem must be faced that it is naturalism which the popular audience demands, and that to offer a naturalistic production of Sophocles or Racine is to invite disaster. Some way of bridging the gap must be found.

I am arguing, therefore, that the acceptable formality and artificiality of the marionette offers one solution to the problem. By presenting the plays in a medium which is itself at a remove from reality, one can make the non-realistic attitudes and conventions of the plays themselves more immediately acceptable. In the following pages I suggest several special applications of this theory—even that, in the case of the Greek theatre, the device of the miniature performance can be used to recreate the scale of the original, and that the spectator, by this means, can be restored to the physical position of his ancient counterpart, with the various important consequences that this entails. I know that this is a solution which will not be acceptable to some. I put it forward in the knowledge that it has been acceptable to many. For the last seventeen years— ten in Great Britain, and seven in the United States and Canada—I have offered a repertoire of plays ranging in time from the Greeks to Racine, and in mood from Sophocles to Plautus. I have played before audiences of all kinds, from high schools and youth clubs to the American Council of Learned Societies; and it is their almost uniformly enthusiastic response that has encouraged me to continue in this work for so long, and finally to commit some of my views to paper.

To this extent, the book is aimed at those who are interested more in the theatre and less, if at all, in marionettes. I hope that it will also have something to say to those who are interested more in marionettes than in the history of the theatre. It makes no pretence, however, at being a technical treatise. The basic techniques of constructing and painting puppets, and of making and lighting a stage, have been described often enough elsewhere, and much better than anything I could write.* My avoidance of technical description does, however, stem partly from another cause. A mediocre technician myself, I am constantly impressed by the accomplishments of others in construction and manipulation, and no less dismayed by the trivial material on which these feats are so often wasted. It seems to me that many puppeteers are so preoccupied with technique that they have lost all sense of what their art should be about. I recently spent some time in discussion with an American puppeteer. She described, in great detail, a puppet ballet that she and her colleagues were creating, and the trouble they had in constructing a puppet dancer who could remove a veil. After six months of experiment, they had eventually achieved an action that was almost completely naturalistic. I was tempted to reply, but did not, that if this was what they wanted it would have been far easier to have used human beings in the first place.

Throughout this book I have tried continually to insist that the true values of the puppet only appear when one accepts it for what it is, and does not try to make it into what it is not, a human being in miniature. Where I have dealt in technical matters, it has only been to point out some modification of accepted practice that I have been forced to make in order to perform the plays that interest me. So far as practicing puppeteers are concerned, I hope that this book may suggest to

---

* For a list of books dealing with technique, as well as other books about puppets, see the Selected Bibliography, pp. 151-152.

them a number of areas of potential material easily adaptable to their purposes, and of somewhat greater dramatic interest than the customary puppet repertoire.

One of the first accounts of puppetry that I read, while still a small boy, was a section in one of those delightful Victorian compendia called *A Thousand and One Things for the Busy Boy to Do*. After the usual instructions on how to construct puppets and stages, the writer touched on material. "Confine yourself to comedy," he stated. "Tragedy is ridiculous on the two-foot boards." Even at that age—and I had scarcely begun to dabble in a medium which already seemed to me full of promise and excitement—this narrow dogmatism repelled me. As I grew older, and began seeking audiences for my work, I found that this attitude was widespread. In Great Britain, my most bitter opponent was tradition—the deeply rooted feeling that puppets were not, and could never be, any more than light entertainment. In the United States I have never encountered this feeling to anywhere near the same extent. On the contrary, I have found in almost every case a willingness to admit that serious puppetry might be possible, and a desire to see it in practice. If one is to conduct one's experiments in public, as in theatre one is bound to do, it seems to me that in spite of the harsh things said from time to time about American popular indifference towards the new in art, I should have to look hard to find audiences more willing to be stimulated, or more interested in new ideas and possibilities, than those with which the United States, particularly in its schools and colleges, has so often provided me.

# Puppets Then and Now

To look for the origin of puppets we should have to go back beyond the beginnings of recorded history. Who was the first man to make a replica of some human or animal figure, and give it jerky motion by means of rods or strings? Puppetry, like part of the drama itself, probably arose from magic and ritual. As man became more civilized, dummies were introduced in place of the human sacrifices of primitive ceremonies, just as in Republican Rome, where a straw figure was cast into the Tiber in recollection of the time when the victim had been a man alive and struggling. Then there were the images of the gods, objects of veneration to the people. It would be a simple and natural step to articulate these figures and create an illusion of life. We know of many cases where the priests, whether for pious or for venal reasons, caused the statue of the god to turn its head, raise its arms, and even speak, to fill the hearts of credulous worshippers with terror and adulation.

As entertainment puppets are at least as old as the theatre itself. Plato mentions what are almost certainly glove-puppets. The first puppeteer known to us by name is Potheinos, a Greek who performed in the great Theatre of Dionysus at

Athens, former home of Aeschylus and Aristophanes. One
ancient commentator notes this as the theatre's ultimate degra-
dation. Medieval puppets enacted religious drama in the
churches, at first as an adjunct to the priestly performers but
remaining long after the live actors had taken their plays into
the streets, and expelled only by the sterner sense of propriety that came with the Reformation. Even in the theatre's
dark ages the puppet tradition has survived, carried from
country to country, adopting new manners, speech, and
techniques, but always giving delight. Its basic and most
popular form has endured through the centuries. Characters
are simple and well-defined types; the figures themselves are
grotesque caricatures; humor is broad, relying more on slapstick and knockabout than on verbal wit. The child who
watches a fairground Punch and Judy is heir to a theatrical
tradition that goes back through the strolling improvisers of
the Commedia dell'Arte, through the pompous doctor, nagging wife and boastful soldier of Roman comedy to the
crude mimes of the early Mediterranean world. Similarly,
the traditional Turkish shadow show whose central character
is Karaghiozis, a character very similar to Punch, is argued
by some scholars to have descended directly from the wandering players who took the later Greek comedy on fit-up
stages to the East. Today it has returned to its home. Karaghiozis showmen have penetrated Greece, and their traditional performances, with grotesque figures capering against
a lamplit screen, have become a familiar and well-loved entertainment in the small towns and villages.

But puppet history, a fascinating subject with many surprising connotations and well worthy of a scholar's attention,
lies outside the scope of this book. The curious reader will do
well to consult George Speaight's *History of the English
Puppet Theatre*, where much of the evidence for the English-speaking world is assembled, together with a summary of
historical origins. Two episodes, however, will be dealt with

here, not so much for what they have to say about puppets as for what they say about the audience. They demonstrate only too clearly the English attitude to puppetry—an attitude which does not appear to have changed to any great degree over the centuries, and to which the United States has fallen heir.

The seventeenth and eighteenth centuries saw the puppet's heyday. With Charles II restored to his father's throne, the theatre came once more into prominence. Reacting from Puritan restrictions, the upper classes swarmed into the playhouses, where playwrights and actors were kept busy pandering to their craving for amusement. Plays were for the most part shallow, bawdy things, tales of domestic intrigue and gay infidelity, but warm, witty, and alive. The puppet theatre shared in this renaissance.

Pepys, that tireless recorder, testifies to the great popularity of puppets at this time. He was himself a keen puppet-goer, visiting the same show more than once, though he is occasionally moved to voice a conventional note of disapproval. In 1614 Ben Jonson had introduced puppets into the action of his satirical comedy *Bartholemew Fair*. Their little play was a burlesque of the classical story of Hero and Leander. The ancient characters are transplanted to a contemporary setting; Leander has himself ferried across the Thames instead of swimming the Hellespont, and drinks with Hero in a London tavern. Cupid plays barman and mixes a love potion in their ale. The puppet play is interrupted by a Puritan, who denounces the show as immoral, but he is soon worsted in argument by one of the puppets. We learn from Pepys that in recent representations this scene had been omitted out of deference to Puritan sentiment. On September 7, 1661, he writes: "And here was 'Bartholemew Fayre' with the puppet show acted today, which had not been these forty years (it being so satyricall against Puritanism, they durst not do it till now, which is strange they should already dare to do it, and the King do countenance it) but I do never a whit like it the better for the puppets, but rather the worse." But two months later he was there again: "My wife and I to 'Bartholemew Fayre' with puppets, which I had seen once before, and the play without puppets often, but though I love the play as much as ever I did, yet I do not like the puppets at all, but think it to be a lessening of it."

Pepys' disapproval did not prevent him from visiting other puppet shows. On May 9, 1662, he writes of one at Covent Garden: "Thence to see an Italian puppet-play that is within the rayles there, the best that ever I saw and great resort of gallants." A few days later he was back with his wife: "My wife and I to the puppet-play in Covent Garden, which I saw the other day, and indeed it is very pleasant. Here among the fiddlers I first saw a dulcimer played on with sticks knocking of the strings, and it is very pretty." On October 8 this show had a command performance; it was acted before King Charles himself, and Pepys, of course, was there.

Towards the end of the year he had found something else to amuse him. "Taking my wife up, carried her to Charing Cross, and there showed her the Italian motion, much after the nature of what I showed her a while since in Covent Garden. Their puppets here are somewhat better, but their motions not at all." In 1663 he "carried them into a puppet play in Lincolnes Inn Fields, where there was the story of Holofernes and other clockwork, very well done." In a note for September 21, 1668, the moralist once again takes control: "To Southwarke-Fair, very dirty, and there saw the puppet-show of Whittington, which was very pretty to see; and how that idle thing do work upon people that see it, and even myself too!"

These entries demonstrate well the nature of puppet production at the time. The stories were simple biblical themes or popular tales, but elaborately mounted with full orchestral accompaniment, and fashionable enough to attract the attention of royalty. More revealing still are Pepys' own comments on the effect these shows had on him. How well he epitomizes the eternal English attitude to puppet theatre—always willing to go, always fascinated by the little figures, and always refusing to take them seriously.

Moving on to the beginning of the eighteenth century, we find an even more striking illustration. The celebrated actor-manager Colley Cibber collaborated with Sir John Vanbrugh to write *The Provoked Husband*, a witty comedy of manners and polite intrigue in the familiar pattern. It was produced in 1728 and published in the same year. Twenty-one years later Henry Fielding wrote his picaresque novel *Tom Jones*. Although prevented from writing his stage satires by the new censorship, Fielding retained his interest in all things theatrical, and chapter twelve of *Tom Jones* tells how a traveling puppet show performed at the inn where the hero had put up for the night. The showman makes the customary boasts, that his figures are "the finest which the world has ever·produced" and that they have given "great satisfaction to all the quality in every town in England." Then the play begins, and it turns out to be none other than the same *Provoked Husband* which had delighted London audiences a score of years before.

The debate which follows is worth quoting at some length.

It was indeed a very grave and solemn entertainment, without any low wit or humour or jests; or, to do it no more than justice, without anything which could provoke a laugh. The audience were all highly pleased. A grave matron told the master she would bring her two daughters the next night, as he did not show any stuff; and an attorney's clerk and an exciseman both declared that the characters of lord and lady Towneley were well preserved, and highly in nature.

The puppet-master was pleased, and launched out on a theory of his art.

He said "The present age was not improved in any thing so much as in their puppet-shows; which, by throwing out Punch and his wife Joan, and such idle trumpery, were at last brought to be a rational entertainment. I remember" said he "when I first took to the business, there was a great deal of low stuff that did very well to make folks laugh; but was never calculated to improve the morals of young folk, which certainly ought to be principally aimed at in every puppet-show: for why may not good and instructive lessons be conveyed this way, as well as any other? My figures are as big as the life, and they represent the life in every particular; and I question not but people rise from my little drama as much improved as they do from the great!"

The audience then discusses among itself the relative merits of the live and the puppet representations.

"Right, friend" cries the clerk, "you are very right. Always avoid what is low. There are several of my acquaintance in London, who are resolved to drive everything which is low from the stage." "Nothing can be more proper," cries the exciseman, pulling his pipe from his mouth. "I remember," added he "(for then I lived with my Lord) I was in the footman's gallery, the night when this play of the Provoked Husband was acted first. There was a great deal of low stuff in it about a country gentleman come up to town to stand for parliament-man; and there they brought a parcel of his servants upon the stage, his coachman I remember particularly; but the gentlemen in our gallery could not bear anything so low, and they damned it. I observe, friend, you have left all that matter out, and you are to be commended for it."

Here we have one of those rare instances where the live stage and its miniature have come into direct contact; where the puppet theatre turns from its traditional low comedy to material written by professional dramatists. Although this particular incident may be fictional, there is ample evidence from other sources that Fielding is satirizing a genuine movement of his day. His attitude is the same as that of Pepys; the puppet theatre must be kept in its place, and any attempt to take it seriously must be knocked on the head.

The landlady in *Tom Jones* seems to embody Fielding's own attitude.

> "I remember when puppet-shows were made of good scripture stories, as 'Jephthah's Rash Vow' and such good things, and when wicked people were carried away by the devil. There was some sense in those matters; but as the parson told us last Sunday, nobody believes in the devil now-a-days; and here you bring about a parcel of puppets dressed up like lords and ladies, only to turn the heads of poor country wenches."

Fielding's own objections seem to be based on style rather than on morality, but it is clear that he too dislikes the puppet's incursion into live theatre, and considers its proper place to be with simple folk tales and "Punch and his wife Joan."

This has been the popular view of puppetry in the English-speaking world to this day. Only rarely has the puppet theatre abandoned the safety of its traditional forms to explore new possibilities; only rarely has it ventured to rival the live stage in presenting serious plays by dramatists worthy of attention. In the last century popular melodramas of the day were reproduced in miniature; the puppet stage performed *Maria Marten* and *East Lynne*. We even read of an adaptation of *Othello* played by the Middleton Marionettes, a family troupe with a long history, in the 1880's. But these were by no means typical examples. For the most part puppet shows were confined to the fairground, and their repertoires were in keeping with their environment.

This is largely the case today. Prevailing opinion may be summed up in two articles of faith: that puppetry is for children, and that puppetry and serious drama will not mix. I quote from a contemporary theatrical dictionary:* "Doll plays have been fads in sophisticated European society, but chiefly they have appealed to children and simple adults who live in areas unvisited by actors." This identification with children is a constant source of difficulty to companies trying to lift their programs out of the common rut. Children make a lively and intelligent audience. They are highly critical, with a stern sense of logic and dramatic propriety; they are more demanding than many performers realize, and will not be fobbed off with half-finished work. It is not easy to play to them, and all the more rewarding to elicit a satisfactory response. But it goes without saying that their comprehension is limited. If the play's subject-matter is beyond their understanding they will soon be bored, regardless of whether they are watching puppets or human beings. Puppets are not magic charms that can be guaranteed to amuse a child audience indefinitely, whatever happens. Nevertheless, their parents bring them, no matter what the play's subject, in the firm belief that puppets and children automatically go together.

I have often been embarrassed in this way in my own classical presentations. When performing Plautus' *Menaechmi* to university audiences, I have sometimes been startled to find that many spectators who must know the play well have brought their children, and that a fair part of the audience has been of tender years. *Menaechmi* is a typical example of Roman comedy at its most vigorous—bawdy, boisterous humor with much highly adult innuendo—a play, in fact, from which most parents would ban their children on moral grounds were it performed live. Yet, simply because the actors are puppets, it is considered safe; the children arrive, and, once the first attraction of the moving figures has worn off, sit impatiently through what must be to them tedious and, one can only hope, meaningless dialogue.

* Sylvan Barnet et al., "Puppet," *Aspects of the Drama* (New York: Little, Brown and Co., 1962).

And yet children are unpredictable. One can never dogmatize about their tastes, and may sometimes find a way to their imaginations with the most unlikely material. Some years ago, in England, I was asked to give a school performance of Molière's *Les Fourberies de Scapin*. Most of the audience were old enough to appreciate the play, but the front two rows were filled, ominously, with children of six or seven. The principal noticed my forebodings and explained that it was impossible to leave them without supervision, but that they would be removed by their parents at the first intermission, their normal time for going home. The performance began, and the children were quiet. Came the intermission, and with it the parents. To everyone's surprise the children refused to leave, and the only threat of disturbance came when their mothers tried to remove them by force. One would imagine Molière's sophisticated comedy to be the last thing to appeal to the six-year-old, but appeal it did, and they sat entranced.

But such exceptions are rare. As a general rule it would be good to see parents applying the same criteria to puppet shows as to live performances. Sure of an adult and sympathetic audience, companies might then embark on a more ambitious repertoire. No parent would dream of taking his child to all films or all plays, or expect him to read and enjoy all books irrespective of their contents; why should this medium prove the exception? We must blame the popular equation of puppets with dolls, a term frequently used by the general public and guaranteed to make any self-respecting puppeteer squirm.

Generally speaking, puppet and live theatre have gone their separate ways, and few have attempted to reconcile them or see how one may illumine the other. The Greek New Comedy, as has already been mentioned, exercised a strong influence on the Turkish shadow-play, and in the classical drama of Japan puppet and live theatre found in combination a mutual source of profit; but such concurrences are rare. In

the popular mind puppets remain on the level of pure entertainment and high art is the prerogative of human actors. The
falsity of this conception is evident when we consider the
work of European puppeteers, who maintain the highest artistic standards and compete with the live theatre on its own
level. No one would wish to abolish the traditional forms of
puppet entertainment, or to forget them altogether. We must
have Punch just as we must have Hamlet. Each is, in his own
way, irreplaceable. Yet must we be content with Punch only?
This is to say that there is no theatre but vaudeville, no music
but the popular song, no art but magazine illustrations. Punch
is the Minsky's of puppetry, but where is its Theatre Guild?
We must look to the continent of Europe to find that.

The puppet stage has not lacked theorists. Von Kleist,
Symons, and Craig, to name only three, have written elo-
quent defenses of the medium; their theories will be treated at
greater length in the next chapter. Haydn composed operas
for marionettes, and Maeterlinck, George Sand, and Shaw
have written plays for them. Yet the fact remains that puppetry in the United States and in England is virtually a dead
art, and the blame for this must rest on puppeteers and public
alike.

For there is no doubt that puppetry is fatally easy. There
is an irresistible attraction about these little moving figures.
Even the poorest Punch and Judy show will attract a crowd;
even marionettes mechanically controlled and jigging aim-
lessly in a store window will fill the sidewalk. The child in us
reacts instinctively. But this engenders a certain laziness in
the puppeteer. When the puppet in itself is so attractive, does
it much matter what it does? Thus a vicious circle is created.
The percipient adult comes to realize that he can expect only
a superficial entertainment; like Pepys, he will be intrigued,
but will not consider it necessary to exercise his mind. So the
public expects to be able to bring children, and troupes who
make their living from puppetry are forced to give the public

what it wants. Inevitably, the entertainment offered cannot rise above a certain level.

This is not to say that English and American puppeteers lack accomplishment. Unfortunately, their achievements have been almost entirely technical. The 1920's saw a notable revival of interest, leading in England to the formation of the British Puppet and Model Theatre Guild to give devotees a meeting place and opportunity for the exchange of information. The United States saw similar organizations and a number of individual experiments of genuine artistic merit. Puppetry acquired some sort of respectability. It has invaded the London theatre; it may be seen off Broadway; it is taught in many schools and training colleges, where it has been realized that the combination of skills required presents a practical exercise not easily come by elsewhere. In the British Isles there are several professional companies taking shows throughout the length and breadth of the country. In the United States, because of the very vastness of the territory, activity has necessarily been more regionalized.

In selecting specific companies to illustrate techniques and material I have chosen mostly British examples, not for chauvinistic reasons, but simply because these companies play to a more representative cross-section of the public and best demonstrate the nature of the popular response to this art-form. Few American companies have achieved recognition on the national level, and of these, some have done so for the wrong reasons: witness the extraordinary *Poupées de Paris*, who presented a mechanical Folies Bergères at the Seattle World's Fair in 1962. Some exponents, notably Bill and Cora Baird, have achieved justly earned recognition on television, but this medium presents a different set of problems. One American company which deserves much more serious recognition than it has received is the puppet opera at the Kungsholm Restaurant in Chicago. Here there are nightly presentations of a repertoire ranging from Gilbert and Sullivan to Wagner, per-

formed by rod-puppets in an exquisitely modelled theatre.
Although the choruses are sometimes static, and a tendency
to overplaying, particularly in the comic pieces, is insufficiently repressed, the work in general represents a fascinating
attempt to solve some of the problems of opera production
by aids which only the puppet can offer. It is significant that,
in this theatre, the mechanics of puppet operation are considered of less importance than the total impact of the production, and both figures and setting are integrated into an
artistically satisfying whole.

In Great Britain, craftsmanship and technique are for the
most part impeccable. This can sometimes be a disadvantage.
The best-known company is undoubtedly that of Waldo Lanchester, who has had permanent marionette theatres at Malvern and Stratford-on-Avon. In construction, Lanchester is
probably the greatest perfectionist in England today. His figures are exquisitely carved, realistic in every detail. They are
wonders when at rest, but too often become mere automata
when in motion. So perfect a reproduction leaves nothing to
the imagination. Lanchester's figures are often like the manni-
kins beloved of German clockmakers, versatile but soulless.
One is moved to say "How clever" more often than "How
beautiful." Being so perfect in themselves, they lack dramatic
force; a clumsier, rougher figure will often create a more
vivid effect. Yet the skill of this company has been justly hon-
ored, and as exhibitions of technical virtuosity its performances are justly admired.

Other companies show similar dexterity in construction
and manipulation. One recalls particularly the *tour de force*
of the Lee Marionettes, who show two glove puppets manip-
ulating a marionette disjointing skeleton, and the Green Man
from the Hogarth-Bussell repertoire who dances a wild and
eccentric dance. There is enough skill here to show that puppetry is a demanding art, and technically more, far more, than
a child's pastime.

It is only fair to say, however, that in Great Britain artistic accomplishment is sacrificed to technique. Too often this elaborate craftsmanship is wasted on trivial subjects. The programs of even the best companies tend to fall into the same monotonous pattern, variety bills of independent turns designed solely to display the performer's skill. There is the inevitable concert pianist, a conventional burlesque in the Paderewski manner, who plays through a Rachmaninov prelude with exaggerated twirls and flourishes. There is the circus, with strong man, sea lion, and assorted clowns—collapsing clowns, tumbling clowns, clowns on stilts. There is the opera singer, usually with an extending neck, who warbles an aria from Verdi or Donizetti. There are dancers by the score, who can mimic the exact steps of ancient and modern dances—to leave England for a moment, one recalls with particular pleasure in this connection the Jamaican figures of Podrecca's Teatro dei Piccoli, who go with unfailing precision through a long and complex rumba. There is the disjointing skeleton. Many of these were stock turns in the fairground booths of the last century; there has been little real artistic advance. The puppeteers are saying "Here is a highly developed, ingenious mechanism. See how cleverly we use it." They should be asking "What can we use it for?"

Several bold experiments stand out from this preoccupation with technique. John Wright, who usually contrives to give the familiar turns a clever and original twist, has produced Molière; his evocative figures for the film *Tales of Hoffman* have also made him widely known. Wright is one of the few artist-craftsmen, but even he is hampered by his public. The Lanchesters themselves have occasionally ventured into the lesser-known byways of chamber opera. In 1949 they produced *L'Amfiparnaso*, by Orazio Vecchi, under the title of *Crabbed Age and Youth*. Written in 1594, *L'Amfiparnaso* epitomizes the spirit of the Commedia dell'Arte with its stock characters—irascible old man, young lovers, scheming servant, learned doctor, bombastic captain. Marionettes are ideally suited to such stylized type-comedy; miming to the New English Singers, the Lanchester figures caught the delicious artificiality of the form. The production pleased both the musical cognoscenti and the general public, who were led by this means to discover the beauties of a hitherto neglected work.

More recently the Lanchesters have performed Haydn's marionette opera *Philemon and Baucis*, the score of which has only lately been restored. This tells the classical story of the old couple who entertained gods in disguise, and were duly rewarded for their pains. Unfortunately, this production was less successful, and met with a cool reception from the London critics. The main fault was perhaps the Lanchesters' insistence on mechanical perfection already mentioned. Their characters were fitted with moving mouths which, as the critics were quick to point out, rarely coincided with the words they were supposed to be singing, and the whole production was too ponderous for the delicacy of Haydn, especially an elaborate cloud which carried the gods down to earth and was only too obviously illuminated from within by electric bulbs. It was a courageous venture, but lacked the sensitivity and grace necessary to convert the audience to serious appreciation.

One other venture of the Lanchesters must not go unrecorded here. In 1949, in a praiseworthy attempt to bring the dramatist back into the puppet theatre, Bernard Shaw was asked to write a play for marionettes. This courage deserved both a better play and a better presentation. Shaw obliged with *Shakes versus Shav*, a fantasy based on his half-serious claim to rival Shakespeare as a playwright. Both dramatists appeared as marionettes, together with Rob Roy, Macbeth, and characters from *Heartbreak House*. The rival claims were argued in near-surrealist fashion; Macbeth's head was struck off in a duel, and the puppet Shaw declaimed "Out, out, brief candle" as he blew out a naked electric bulb which descended from the flies. Although amusing enough, the piece was little more than a music-hall sketch, and the dialogue, abominably recorded by members of the Malvern Festival Company, was at times almost incomprehensible. Here was a precious chance wasted; one could sense the relief with which the audience returned to the more conventional fare of dancing turnips and underwater ballet.

In their more serious pieces the Lanchesters' chief failing is their inability to see the production as a whole. The recorded sound seems to have no relation to the stage picture. Even in their *Peter and the Wolf*, an evocation of Prokofiev's well-known orchestral fairytale—given with much more sensitivity by the Bairds in the United States—the puppet action proceeds independently of the music, without any attempt at the stylization and rhythmic movement that it so obviously demands. We have only to remember Walt Disney's treatment of the piece in *Make Mine Music* to realize the tremendous possibilities for puppets here. In the film, the cartoon characters were balletic conceptions; every phrase of the score had its visual counterpart. If the Lanchesters would simplify their over-detailed figures and concentrate more on production, they would perhaps arouse the response that their experiments deserve.

One of the most important enterprises of recent years has been the Hogarth Puppets' production of Kingsley's *The Water Babies* in London. Here Jan Bussell and Ann Hogarth abandoned their conventional repertoire (they invented, among other things, a singularly repellent television character called Muffin the Mule) for a new type of Christmas entertainment. The story, an allegorical fairy tale with underwater scenes and magical transformations, is one that is fully possible only to marionettes. In many ways it is the perfect compromise for a puppet troupe that wants to proceed to higher things. There are enough characters, and enough moments of simple and obvious humor, to keep a young audience amused, while at the same time the underlying social theme makes a serious claim on adult attention. Hailed as the first full-length marionette play to be performed in London for many years, its success provoked discussion on the principles of marionette production, and on puppetry as an art form, in so staid a journal as *The Oxford Magazine*.

But the Hogarths' greatest artistic achievement is probably their exquisite shadow show, played as one item in their normal variety performances. Bussell uses a small translucent screen set into the proscenium above the main stage opening and colored, transparent figures after the manner of the traditional Javanese shadow-shows. The figures are designed by Lotte Reiniger, the German artist well known in this country for her shadow films, who has also considerably influenced Bussell's technique. They are held against the screen and operated by rods; the lighting is so cunningly arranged that these controls are hardly seen.

The technique owes much to film. There are several puppets for each character in different sizes to give the effect of varying perspectives. Alternating between close-up and long-shot, the medium has many of the advantages of film cartoon, but with more delicate color and an immediate actor-audience response that the film does not allow. Every effect is achieved by the simplest and most direct means; there is no striving after mechanical surprises. When a storm is required, a blue color filter interposed between lamp and screen is shaken to produce an undulating pattern of colored light and shade. Bussell is adventurous in his choice of material. One play is based on Oscar Wilde's *The Happy Prince*, a moral fairy tale of the richly decorated statue of a prince that uses a swallow as its emissary to strip it of its gold and jewels and take them to the poor. Winter comes, the swallow dies of cold, and the prince's leaden heart cracks in two. The story is read by a narrator and illustrated by the tinted shadows moving across the tiny screen. In its miniature perfection it recaptures all the art of the East; yet, to the general public, the Hogarths are known only for their vastly inferior children's performances, which television has raised to a point in the public esteem far exceeding their merits.

On a smaller scale Olive Blackham has investigated the possibilities of marionettes in such diverse drama-forms as the Japanese No theatre and Chekhov. She uses simple, highly stylized figures, sometimes with nothing more than a square block to represent a man's head, a wooden ball for a woman's. The play is more important than the puppet; it is enough if only the general idea is presented, and the rest left to the audience's imagination. These experiments, not widely enough seen, represent puppetry at its purest and best.

Let us now leave the British scene and look elsewhere. Here we are conscious at once of a fundamental difference of approach. Puppetry on the Continent, and especially in Germany, Austria, and Czechoslovakia, has a long and honorable history. There are numerous permanent theatres, in some cases with state support. Puppetry is recognized as an art form in its own right. The theatres play to adult audiences and are paid the compliment of detailed and serious criticism. The result is a far higher level of artistic achievement; puppetry becomes a medium for political and social satire, for high tragedy and comedy, for opera, ballet, and burlesque.

The Italian company previously referred to, Podrecca's Teatro dei Piccoli, "the theatre of the little people," is popular both in its own country and abroad. It made the first of several visits to England in 1923, and has more recently visited the United States. Of all European companies it is perhaps the one most closely allied to the English-speaking tradition. Podrecca's repertoire is composed of short turns and tableaux, inspired by travels over the greater part of the world. He uses a stage large enough to occupy a full-size theatre, and numerous operators. His programs have a grandeur of conception that English-speaking companies have only rarely achieved.

Podrecca reveals a characteristically Italian love of spectacle, at once his greatest strength and his greatest weakness. Several items are elaborate mixtures of song and dance, involving large numbers of figures against a lavish scenic background which usually makes its own contribution to the action. One such scene is a conventional evocation of the American Deep South. A chorus of banjo-strumming Negroes and cotton-picking mammies sing traditional plantation songs. As the light slowly fades a paddle-steamer, gay with colored lanterns, sails majestically up the river behind them. It is a simple scene, hackneyed perhaps and with no dramatic content, but beautifully presented.

The trouble is that these spectacular scenes tend to be repetitive. Although different in dress and atmosphere, they are all built on the same plan. There is little difference between the Mississippi scene and a chorus of Italian folk-dancers, though in the latter case the paddleboat is replaced by an erupting volcano. Sometimes this use of spectacle degenerates into mere display. *Snow White*, which begins simply and charmingly by recounting the old fairy tale, ends in a riot of color. Snow White joins the dwarfs in a wild dance; whirling rabbits emerge from the bushes, leaves fall, huge butterflies circle over their heads. Suddenly the lights fade and behold! everything is luminous. The stage becomes a lurid kaleidoscope, certainly impressive but quite out of keeping with the earlier part of the scene.

In his love of spectacle and his willingness to go to any lengths to achieve a magnificent effect, Podrecca is the Billy Rose of marionette showmen. He can occasionally surprise with a moment of real beauty. In one scene, inspired by his visit among the Andean peasants, there is a dance of South American Indians. A file of gaily cloaked dancers advances across the stage to a persistent drum rhythm, now advancing, now retreating in simple ritual movements. Then the stage is empty, and a solitary figure appears, again in striped cloak and sombrero, leading a llama. He carries a flute. Lifting it to his mouth he begins to play, and the llama paces in time to the music. Slowly the forestage lights dim, and the backcloth glows red with the color of the setting sun. The peasant and his llama are seen as silhouettes against the darkening background. The pure notes of the flute rise and fall, the llama's steps become slower, his head droops as he grows weary; and then, in a moment of haunting beauty as the two figures stand motionless against the last of the dying light, the curtain falls. This is a revue number carried into the realms of poetry.

For even finer things we must turn from Italy to Russia and Austria. The visits of Professor Sergei Obraztsov, Director of the Central State Puppet Theatre of Soviet Russia, first to Great Britain and more recently to the United States, have been revelations both to the general public and to professional puppeteers. Obraztsov is a highly accomplished artist in his own right. Alone on a bare stage, he can give life and movement to the simplest figures. Several of his turns are performed single-handed, with the most rudimentary glove-puppets. These, with their limited range of movement, are notoriously the most difficult figures to use well, but in his hands they become infinitely versatile. A bulbous-nosed plastic head pulled over one hand becomes a drunkard, singing as he refreshes himself with copious draughts, growing more and more maudlin, and winking evilly as he empties the bottle. Or Obraztsov can rock a puppet baby to sleep in his arms with such tenderness that it becomes a laughing, crying, wriggling child before our eyes, and we forget that it is hollow, given animation by one hand and arm alone.

The rest of the Theatre's repertoire is more elaborate, played on a full stage with lavish three-dimensional settings. For full-length plays Obraztsov uses rod-puppets, developed from the traditional techniques of the Far East but here brought to mechanical perfection. Operators stand beneath the high stage, concealed from view by a curtain and controlling the puppets above their heads by rods hidden in the bodies and clothing. Several operators may be needed for complicated movements. In the satirical fantasy *An Extraordinary Concert*, a tango-dancing couple requires six men to work it. Rod puppets have a precision of movement difficult to achieve in other forms; this makes them peculiarly suitable for pathos. *Aladdin* has several such moments. When the hero is captured by his enemies and chained in a prison cell his head droops, his arms stretch out behind him as if he would thrust the confining walls away, his whole body expresses the dejection of captivity and the longing for flight. This is enhanced by subtle illumination, a dramatic interplay of highlights and shadows equalling the lighting resources of any live theatre. Operators are trained as highly as ballet dancers to work in a team, and their movements are a choreographic pattern in themselves; the result is evident in the superb coordination of the figures.

Obraztsov distinguishes carefully between the requirements of child and adult entertainment. For the youngest age-group he puts on short two-act plays with simple subject matter. These plays are usually fairy tales, and care is taken to eliminate any matter which might frighten or distress the very young. Fantasies and fairy tales are also enjoyed by adult audiences, but here the manner is more sophisticated, with strong dramatic action as well as the magic tricks and transformations that puppets can do so well. In *Aladdin* the magic palace rises tier by tier from the ground. Other plays are Carlo Gozzi's *Reindeer King*, which is sometimes performed live in this country, and a dramatization of Gogol's story *Christmas Eve*. But for the most part, adult material takes the form of social satire. One of the most popular plays is *Two-Love to Us*, a witty attack on the modern mania for sport. Here the puppets skate, sail, and play tennis.

Significantly, it is in the field of satire that the puppet theatre seems to have established its widest adult appeal. Puppets lend themselves obviously and easily to caricature, and in Italy and Eastern Europe have often been used as political weapons. Equally significantly, and more sadly, the appearance of Obraztsov's subtly satirical *Extraordinary Concert* on American television was preceded by a long and anxious announcement by Ed Sullivan; he explained that although this entertainment was intended primarily for children, it was hoped that some adults might condescend to watch it too.

Obraztsov's effect on his English-speaking audiences may be seen in the rapturous reception given him by the critics. The *Times Educational Supplement* of London wrote of his "irresistible demonstrations of puppetry as a highly adult and subtle art. Sentimentality, pretentiousness, and sensation-hunting were among the evils caught in his fine web of ridicule." *Theatre Arts* devoted a long article to his work. Seen by a wider audience on television, his performances gave many their first insight into the wider possibilities of this fascinating medium.

From Russia to Austria and Hermann Aicher's Marionette Theatre at Salzburg, Herr Aicher has an international reputation and now performs abroad more often than in his own city; but surely his work may be seen at its best in the perfect setting of Salzburg itself, where thousands assemble annually for the Mozart Festival, where the glockenspiel chimes out the composer's tunes above the narrow, crowded streets and the tiny marionette theatre is as much part of the scene as the great Festival Hall itself. For, like Salzburg, the Marionette Theatre is mainly devoted to Mozart and his works. While the rest of the repertoire would alone command respect— Shakespeare's *Tempest*, Strauss's *Fledermaus*, the fairy tales of *Snow White* and *The Sleeping Beauty*, and exquisite ballets—it is in the operas that the company's genius truly reveals itself. Herr Aicher performs both major and minor works—*Apollo and Hyacinth, Bastien and Bastienne, La Finta Giardiniera, The Impresario, Don Giovanni,* and *The Magic Flute.* It is on the last that the Theatre's fame chiefly rests.

Mozart wrote *The Magic Flute* in 1791 to the libretto of Emanuel Schikaneder, who wanted a fairy tale with strong spectacular appeal. Mozart, of course, contrived to create something far deeper, but the staging of the opera has been a perpetual problem in the live theatre, involving as it does so many changes and trick effects. Prince Tamino, the hero, is rescued from a serpent by the Three Ladies, servants of the Queen of Night. Their mistress charges him to rescue her daughter, who is imprisoned in the temple of Sarastro, the High Priest. He is aided in his mission by the comic Papageno, a bird catcher who is himself half bird, by the magic flute which gives the opera its title, and by a magic chime of bells. He soon discovers that it is Sarastro who is truly good and the Queen who is evil; together he and the Princess pass through the ordeals of fire and water and enter a new world of happiness.

Few live theatres are equipped to deal adequately with the effects required. Often many of these effects are omitted, or so curtailed that the opera becomes little more than a concert performance. But these problems vanish with marionettes; on so small a scale all things are possible. Herr Aicher uses an unusually deep stage, only a third of which is normally occupied with action; the rest houses the simple, beautiful, and constantly changing settings against which the marionettes perform. He creates an Egypt—or rather, an enchanted world with Egyptian affinities—of mist-wrapped mountains through which the hideous serpent crawls; of stylized forests; of looming temples and pyramids. The Queen of Night swoops down on a silver crescent moon, and the skies darken at her approach. Papageno is not the usual singer in feathered costume, but truly half man and half bird. Pamina, the Princess, sits prisoner in the curved bars of a gilded cage. When Tamino plays the magic flute, curious birds and beasts come out to dance—an ostrich, a pelican, a shaggy lion, even three diminutive penguins.

So much for Schikaneder; but Mozart is not neglected. Herr Aicher is not blind to the deeper symbolism of the work, and achieves a grandeur which fully expresses the eternal conflict between Light and Darkness, Good and Evil. This is aided by the skillful use of gauze screens to increase the effect of majesty and distance, and by adjusting the sizes of the figures in relation to their background. In the first Temple scene there are huge doors at each side of the forestage from which walls in false perspective lead back to a third door, small as though seen at a great distance. It is flung open; behind it an even smaller figure appears. Thus, by constructing not only the setting but the characters in false perspective, all restrictions of space are abolished, and the action is taken outside the limits of the marionette stage into the realm of infinite distance.

This production is perhaps the most striking modern example of how the techniques of puppetry may be applied to works originally conceived for the live theatre. Herr Aicher uses many of the traditional tricks, and the accepted modes of puppet behavior. What distinguishes him from other workers in the field is that he does not use them for their own sake, but subordinates everything to the conception of the work as a whole. Perfectly synchronized to the recording of an earlier Festival production, the Salzburg Marionette Theatre's *Magic Flute* is at least equal, and in many ways superior, to the finest live performance, for every element is designed to catch the essential spirit of Mozart.

This survey of some of the leading contemporary companies shows that puppetry, in competent hands, can be taken far out of the sphere of nursery entertainment to become an art form in its own right, no less valuable a means of expression than the live theatre. Some years ago a member of a certain school board was reported as objecting to the teaching of puppetry in schools on the ground that it was no more than "dangling dolls on bits of string." By the same token we could reduce all painting to daubing pigment on canvas, all music to blowing and plucking. Puppetry is an artistic medium like any other. It is only a means to an end, and whether the end is a masterpiece or a triviality rests with the calibre of the artist. The examples given above show how different national and individual characteristics find in puppetry the vehicle for self-expression, whether the work takes the form of music-hall, sophisticated cabaret, spectacle, satire, or the reinterpretation of existing masterpieces. There is no set form of puppet entertainment to which all puppeteers must subscribe. Aicher and Obraztsov, who both use puppets, no more resemble each other than Watteau and Braque, who both use paints.

The puppet should be a servant, not a master, a means to an end rather than an end in itself. The puppet will do whatever it is told, become whatever its maker wishes; it is all the more important to tell it the right things. When dissatisfied with a live performance we often find it difficult to apportion the blame. We say "It was a good play, but badly acted," or "The set was interesting, but the costumes were dreadful." The puppeteer who makes and operates his own figures, who produces, sets, and dresses the play, must take all the praise and blame on his own head. As in painting, design and execution must go hand in hand. What we see on the stage is a manifestation of the puppeteer himself; in the puppets he lays bare his own soul.

It is essential, then, that the puppeteer should put first things first. As in the live theatre, he should begin by selecting worthy material and then devote his talents to interpreting it, not start with his figures and only afterwards look for things for them to do. A strong script will always compensate for weak technique, but the most brilliant technique cannot make trivia more than trivial.

This choice of material is currently the puppet theatre's greatest difficulty. Few serious writers have considered the medium worthy of their attention, and most plays written specifically for puppets are puerile, devoid of literary or dramatic interest. One of the aims of this book is to overcome this difficulty by showing some of the ways in which puppetry can be used to interpret the live drama. Here are innumerable works of acknowledged merit; anyone who admits the possibilities of puppetry will welcome the challenge of testing them in this way. In measuring puppets against the yardstick of serious dramatic accomplishment one may learn what they can do, and, more important, what they cannot do; one may learn their power and beauty, the wide possibilities that they offer to the creative artist in the theatre, and the ways in which they can move an audience to tears, terror, or laughter.

This book does not aim to lay down any hard and fast rules. Many things can be learned only by constant practice and experiment; many of the best results, as in any art, come about by happy accident. It is intended only to suggest a few general principles as to the right sort of play to choose, and to record one man's work with marionettes in the field of classical drama.

# The Puppet and the Play

$B$y this time the reader is probably saying "Yes, this is all very well. The people you write of can no doubt produce beautiful things. But they have all the resources of a permanent theatre—money, space, skilled craftsmen, qualified engineers, scene-painters, electricians, and recording equipment. How can I, working on a small scale with limited means, hope to achieve anything comparable to this?"

This is a natural and common objection. The amateur puppeteer, pursuing his hobby in his own home, may well feel that he is not equipped for adventure and experiment, and that these things are the prerogative of larger and professionally organized companies. But experience has shown that this is not so. Those who earn their living by puppetry must satisfy the public demand, and so are to a large extent compelled to be conservative. As so often in other branches of the performing arts, it is only the amateur who can safely afford to experiment, to explore new forms and techniques, and to run the risk of failure.

Nor are technical resources always important. They can even be a liability. Art, it has been wisely said, is not addition but subtraction; what you leave out is more important than what you put in. In puppetry, as in every art, the guiding principle is simplicity. It is only necessary to have a firm grasp of essentials and the power of self-criticism. If the work is to have its effect, anything inessential must be rigorously excluded, and in this respect material limitations may well be an advantage. Herr Aicher's success with his Mozart productions does not depend on elaborate technical resources—many theatres are larger and more lavishly equipped than his—but on his determination to put Mozart first and technique second. Any stage trick or clever piece of business, however delightful in itself, is rejected if it contributes nothing to the understanding of the opera.

If the puppeteer finds something worth expressing and goes about the simplest way to express it, he will not be far wrong. Here the amateur, the individual working on a small scale, will often find himself at an advantage. Simplicity will be forced on him by lack of means, where someone better provided might fall into the trap of over-elaboration. We often find that Shakespeare performed by children or by amateurs is more directly moving than a full production by professionals; the latter tend to be so concerned with technique that they sacrifice meaning and poetry, so swamped in stage mechanics that they forget about the play. In puppetry the very lack of resources may lead at once to an effect which a more lavishly equipped theatre would discover only after much trial and error. A story from the live theatre illustrates this. A Broadway director was working on a scene in which thousands of dead souls had to be seen passing over a river. He experimented with all the scenic and light resources of his vast stage, but in vain; he could find nothing convincing. At last, on the point of giving up in despair, he found, almost by accident, that a simple strip of gauze, lit in a certain way, would give exactly the effect he wanted. A stock company working on a limited budget and always forced to find the cheapest way out would probably have hit on this solution at once.

Technique is necessary, but should never be allowed to dominate the work. It is something to be acquired in practice. Many new ways of doing things will suggest themselves with the widening of experience. Learn them and master them, but never let them master you. Never do something merely because it is clever, or obviously difficult. Never, on the other hand, be afraid of something merely because it seems difficult. As long as there is a clear idea of what should be done, a way of doing it will usually be found, and the simplest way is always the best.

In the first chapter the genus *puppet* and the species *marionette* have been referred to indiscriminately. It may be as well at this point to define the various classes, and say something about their capabilities. *Puppet* is the general term for any replica of a human, animal, or other form moved by artificial means. The word presupposes human control. Clockwork figures and similar automata are not, strictly speaking, puppets. There are four main types of puppets, each with its own peculiar advantages and drawbacks.

*Glove-puppets* are by far the simplest to make and use. This type is familiar from the Punch and Judy show. The figures have a hollow head and arms and a long, sleeve-like body; the operator inserts his hand in the body and controls head and arms with his fingers. Being so easy to work, glove-puppets are naturally the most popular with children. But their range of movements is limited, and except in the hands of an expert they are unconvincing in anything but the simplest burlesques. Some puppeteers use nothing else; one of their greatest exponents has been the British Walter Wilkinson, the wandering puppeteer who has tramped all over the country with his shows. But even he is forced to recognize their limitations, and confines his repertoire to simple mimes and ballads. Obraztsov also uses them, but only for short items where their lack of flexibility is not apparent. Glove-puppets are ideal for introducing children and beginners to the basic requirements of construction and control, but lack the interest necessary to sustain a long performance, and are by their nature unsuitable for the higher forms of puppet art.

Second come *shadow-puppets*, the traditional art of the Far East. These are flat figures held against a translucent screen; a light is set behind them, and the audience sees their shadows on the other side. They may be solid, or perforated to give a black-and-white effect, or, like the Javanese figures, have holes covered with colored transparencies to throw a tinted shadow. Jan Bussell has shown what beautiful effects may be created by these means. Lotte Reiniger's shadow-puppet films have also become well known outside her native Germany. The technique for filming is less straightforward: figures are laid on a horizontal ground glass screen and filmed by the "stop-motion" method, in which the camera pauses between frames to allow the figures to be moved. The Karaghiozis tradition in Turkey and Greece has already been described. Here painters and sculptors have often been attracted by the medium, designing both the figures themselves and quaint settings to go with them.

The chief limitation of the shadow-puppet is obvious; it is confined to two dimensions. It is perhaps at its best in illustrating stories read by a narrator, in the manner of a moving picture book. This is the method of the Javanese shows, where long performances are given to a continual chant and loud orchestral accompaniment.

*Rod-puppets* have attracted greater interest since their brilliant exploitation by Obraztsov's company. The method of operation has already been described. Absolute precision of control is possible, and these figures have great dignity and beauty. Their most noteworthy appearance in serious drama in recent years has been in the American production of Stravinsky's *Oedipus Rex*. This dramatic oratorio, with a libretto in Latin by Jean Cocteau, retells Sophocles' tragic drama. Stravinsky visualized his characters as being larger than life-size, and in this production they were represented by huge rod-puppets designed by the leading American puppeteer Remo Bufano. Each was worked by a number of concealed operators. Standing before the massed chorus, moving with sweeping impressive gestures, they symbolized the super-human nature of the drama in a way that no actor could have achieved.

Science has recently invaded this field to produce a modern variant—puppets operated by remote control and responding to magnets moving under the stage. Such figures have been used for a film of *Hansel and Gretel*. But these are dangerously close to automata. The film proved, if anything, how neces-sary it is for the operator to be in direct contact with his puppet. When the human element is removed, the puppet it-self lacks humanity and becomes no more than an ingenious mechanical toy.

It may well be that rod-puppets are the ideal medium for serious drama. Obraztsov has demonstrated how they combine the qualities necessary for both tragedy and comedy. They have almost unrestricted powers of movement, subtlety, and grace. For the amateur, however, and for the individual work-ing with small resources, they present several difficulties. They need a special type of stage, at least head-high to con-ceal the operator, and a larger staff than is usually available.

All in all, *marionettes* are most generally satisfactory, and the most familiar type in use today. These are jointed figures controlled from above by strings or wires, which may be of any number from one to forty depending on the size of the marionette and what it has to do. Although requiring more skill in their construction than glove or shadow puppets, they are not unduly difficult; they can be made in a number of ways, and need be no more complicated than the operator wishes. They combine a wide range of movements with com-parative ease of operation. Once the basic movements have been mastered—walking, sitting, moving the head—the rest follow with surprising speed, and the marionette will quickly assume a personality of its own. The stage, again, can be as simple or as complicated as the operator desires. Some puppeteers use a large stage with a high "bridge"—the platform on which the operators stand to overlook their figures—and elaborate scenic and lighting equipment; others have only a simple curtain background or none at all, with the marionette lit by a single spotlight. Suitable for both tragedy and comedy, marionettes are best for the puppeteer with little space or assistance at his disposal, and it is with marionettes and their potentialities that this book will chiefly deal.

The creative artist in each field must begin by considering the limitations of his medium. A sculptor working in stone tries to utilize the natural qualities of his material, and does not attempt to treat it as if it were wood or bronze. A painter knows that oils and watercolor have different characteristics, and demand different methods. So, in selecting a play for marionettes, we must ask first of all what we may legitimately expect them to do. We would not ask children to act Chekhov, or dancers to sing Puccini. We must treat our marionettes as we would actors, and look for something where their potentialities may be used to the best advantage.

A little thought will suggest that the marionette has two main limitations. The first is imposed by its construction. It is true that the marionette can be made in any shape the maker fancies. It can be anything human or animal; it can be an imaginary monster or an abstract shape. It can be as large or as small as you please, within reason; it can be solid, hollow, or transparent; it can have two heads or six legs; it can shrink, distend itself, come apart; it can move in more than one plane, and fly as well as walk. But, because of the necessary strings stretching up to the operator's hand, it cannot go through doors or arches or under tables. (Rod-puppets present precisely the opposite difficulty; their stage can have doors but no floor.) It cannot change its clothes except with great difficulty, as the strings must penetrate the costume. The string method of control, with the operator at some distance from his puppet, also makes problems in performing tiny gestures; the marionette lacks the rod-puppet's precision. Actions such as drinking and smoking cannot be carried out unless the figure is very carefully designed and weighted.

The second limitation is one of size. Unless one is prepared to have large figures, with the consequent difficulties of weight and portability, anything small or subtle will be lost on the greater part of the audience. A marionette which winks and wiggles its ears is of little use if only the first few rows can see it. The Teatro dei Piccoli has a flute-player who raises his eyebrows and moves each finger on his instrument separately; but he is four feet high, and requires a team of operators to work him. Similarly, it is no use putting fine and detailed work into the features and costumes and relying on these for effect. What looks exquisite at close range will be an indistinguishable blur at twenty feet and invisible at fifty. Movement, dress, and characterization must be bold and striking to carry to the limits of the auditorium. Excessive attention to detail is not only wasteful but positively harmful.

The moral of this is clear. Unless you wish only to provide a mechanical diversion for a handful of spectators, go after broad, sweeping effects and avoid visual subtlety. Sir Henry Irving used to encourage his casts to speak out by telling them to remember the little boy who had paid his pennies to sit at the back of the gallery, and deserved to hear as much as the fashionable audience in the orchestra stalls. This principle holds equally true for marionettes. Show nothing that the furthermost spectator cannot see. Thus we have come back to our earlier counsel of simplicity; the broad and striking effects, the touches that are visible to all, will be those that are simplest and most direct.

We now have some valuable criteria to guide our choice of play. Look doubtfully at anything relying on a pattern of

subtle, complicated, or highly realistic movements. Go instead to plays where only the broadest and most elementary
gestures are required, gestures which cannot be missed or mis-
interpreted at the back of the hall. Avoid plays with realistic
settings—domestic dramas where the characters use doors and
windows, toy with teacups, hide in cupboards. Look for plays
where the setting is open and imaginative, and may be indicated by a few significant features which leave most of the
space free for the action. Strings have a great facility for
catching in the most unlikely places, and as a general rule the
less scenery the better. It is possible, with ingenuity, to make
marionettes perform many realistic actions. It is even possible
to create the illusion that they pass through doors and under
arches, although they cannot actually do so. But here one will
run the risk of so impressing the audience with tricks that a
momentary action unimportant in itself may attract more attention than it deserves, and the balance of the play will suffer
in consequence. Mechanical tricks have a fatal fascination.
While permissible in cabaret or music-hall, where the immediate effect is everything and there is no continuity of
action, they should be regarded with the deepest suspicion in
a play, and admitted only if the desired effect cannot be at-
tained in any other way. An actor would not be allowed to
sing one of his speeches, even if he were another Caruso; a
marionette who displays his tricks unnecessarily will detract
from, not add to, the performance.

In practice this means avoiding the naturalistic drama altogether. It is compounded of all those things that the marionette cannot do. The play's action is based on real life, on
everyday happenings and emotions. Although adjusted to
give coherence and heightened dramatic interest, it still repro-
duces the action of home, office, and street, and the settings
must be naturalistic to correspond. Similarly, naturalistic acting, the type which is most familiar today, is based on the innumerable small, subtle actions of everyday life—clenching

the fist, shifting the foot, drooping the shoulders. To a large extent it relies on the facial expression. Anyone who has watched Sir Laurence Olivier will know how much he uses his face for characterization, and he has said himself that he would sooner lose a hand than one of his eyes.

Marionettes, with their immobile faces, unarticulated hands, and limbs restricted to one or two joints cannot reproduce this range of expression. I have seen a German marionette of Faust with the head so carved that the expression changes under strong directional lighting with the play of highlight and shadow. Seen from one angle the face is joyful, from another gloomy and introspective. But even here the number of moods is limited to two or three. The puppeteer might learn much from modern sculpture, often designed to give different impressions according to the way the light falls; he might also use the trick of an ancient Roman comic mask, which had a frown on one side and a smile on the other, so that the character seemed to change his expression by turning his head. But this is as far as the marionette can go; the more subtle changes are denied him.

True, the audience will often imagine facial expression where none exists. As the marionettes move under stage lighting the shadows change, and imagination does the rest. I have often been asked, when performing marionette opera, how I managed to make the mouths of such small figures move. In fact they did not move at all. Again, a spectator at an oriental rod-puppet tragedy has reported that when the puppet king was mortally wounded and fell dying to the ground, he was prepared to swear that the wooden face turned pale. If marionettes can work on the imagination to such an extent, so much the better. But these things are subjective; they vary with the individual spectator, and it is impossible to rely on them.

In many modern plays the words in themselves are comparatively unimportant. The printed text is less than half the play. The true effect, the essential nuance that makes the dialogue spring to life, is conveyed by gesture and by facial expression. Here the marionette must yield to the live actor. Puppets cannot play Noel Coward. By forcing them into a naturalistic pattern, and insisting that they perform in a way that is unnatural to them, you will make them into no more than mechanical reproductions of the human figure; they will inevitably be inadequate, and the play will be a travesty.

The marionette's great virtue is its power to transcend the limits of human behavior, to present abstractions from life rather than models of it. Shaped at will under its maker's hand, it can capture the essence of the character in its appearance. Where the actor is a photograph, the marionette is a caricature —but in the widest possible sense, sympathetic as well as grotesque, conveying the spirit of the character not only through its features but through significant distortions of its whole body. Jan Bussell has written of a marionette Secret Police Agent, the work of a puppeteer satirist, whose hands end in gun barrels instead of fingers. Here the notion of violence and brutality is conveyed in a way impossible for the live actor. Thus the marionette is a popular medium for political and social satire; it is a cartoon brought to life.

The puppeteer will discover for himself numerous applications of this principle. A glutton can be grotesquely, impossibly fat. An inquisitive character can have ears out of all proportion to his body. A proud and tyrannical king can be shown with huge scepter and crown, the symbols of his rule. A nagging wife's influence over her submissive husband can be demonstrated by their respective sizes.

We may now go on to suggest several types of plays suitable for marionettes. Firstly, the magic play, where characters are required to perform such non-human actions as flying, vanishing, and changing their shape. Aicher's successful realization of the magic element in *The Magic Flute* has already been described. Things which live actors can do only with difficulty and with the aid of mechanical apparatus, and then

only half-convincingly, marionettes can accomplish with perfect simplicity and charm. *Alice in Wonderland* is another
popular subject, for the puppeteer can reproduce Tenniel's
illustrations and the numerous transformations which the
story demands down to the last detail. Sometimes a live actress
is used for Alice in certain scenes. Also popular is Thackeray's
*The Rose and the Ring,* originally written as a sophisticated
fairy tale and since dramatized in several versions. This involves, among other things, a footman who is changed into a
doorknocker and a hideous old countess who turns into a
young and lovely girl. Ogres, dwarfs, giants, all the creatures
of fantasy and fairy tale are the legitimate province of the
marionette.

We may include here plays in which the characters are
animals or other non-human beings. Capek's *The Insect Play*
(*The World We Live In*) comes immediately to mind. In
this social satire various classes of humanity are represented
by types of the insect world—pleasure-seekers by the giddy
butterflies, soulless industrial civilization by the ants. A tramp
wanders among them and ends the play by falling dead in a
ditch, while two languid snails lisp his epitaph. Then there is
Maeterlinck's *The Blue Bird,* a long poetic allegory of two
poor children who wander through the realms of fact and
fantasy, of past, present, and future, in search of the Blue
Bird, symbol of eternal happiness. They are accompanied by
their dog and cat and by such domestic characters as Bread
and Sugar come mysteriously to life. Their journey takes
them to the palace of the Queen of Night, through a forest
of talking trees, and to the land of children as yet unborn.
There is endless scope for the marionette here.

Next, and more important, we may consider plays whose
characters, though human, are not so much real people as
types or abstractions, not individuals but personifications of
certain qualities. A survey of dramatic history reveals many
such. Going back to the earliest times we find that the first

recorded European drama, that of the Greeks, dealt in such abstractions. The characters of Greek tragedy, particularly early tragedy, tend to be symbols, personifications of such qualities as pride, anger, justice, and revenge, rather than fully individualized human beings. The Greek tragedian was not, on the whole, interested in portraying a fully rounded individual with every aspect of his character represented. Only those characteristics which were dramatically relevant were included.

In presenting such characters, the Greek actor had many visual affinities with the marionette. He wore a mask, and so was denied the subtlety of facial expression which is the modern actor's chief stock-in-trade. He wore formal costume which merely suggested his character and in no way realistically represented it. Until fairly late in the period, kings and commoners, warriors, beggars, and priests were all dressed in approximately the same way. Also, he was limited by the size of his theatre and his relationship to the audience. This factor of scale is vital to the understanding of Greek drama, and it is strange that so fundamental a problem should have been so often neglected. Greek theatres were huge. The Theatre of Dionysus at Athens, where the great plays were first performed, held approximately 17,000 spectators. Others, particularly those of the Greek colonies in Asia Minor, were even larger. In such an arrangement the acting area was dwarfed by the auditorium. Visual details would have been lost on a large proportion of the audience. Many of them would have been conscious of the actor only as a colored dot moving against the bleached stone of the theatre. It has been calculated that the spectator in the back row of the Theatre of Dionysus in Athens would see the actor as only three quarters of an inch high.

This problem of scale imposes certain restrictions both on the actor and on the dramatist. A Greek actor could not employ subtle gesture. This would have been lost on most of his audience. Although we know little about the details of Greek acting, we may be fairly sure that the performer would have confined himself to broad and obvious gestures (these would be encouraged, in any case, by the requirements of open-air as contrasted with indoor performance) and that to a modern spectator his pattern of movement would suggest ballet rather than legitimate acting as we now know it. Nor could the author rely on stage business to create his effects. In Greek tragedy, the examples of dramatic points made by business *alone* can be counted on the fingers of one hand. In almost every case the visual point is underlined verbally—the characters tell you what they are doing, as well as actually doing it—to ensure that even the most remote members of the audience will comprehend. It is in words that the Greek tragedian mostly works, and on words he could rely, for in spite of the size of Greek theatres their acoustics were uniformly good and in many places flawless. The audience could always hear, even when it could not see.

In transposing such plays to the modern theatre a number of problems arise. Modern playhouses, roofed and enclosed, are considerably smaller than their Greek counterparts, and therefore more intimate. Even modern open-air theatres rarely approach the Greek size. In such circumstances, the Greek dramatist and his modern audience are placed in a false relationship. Greek tragedy was essentially a long-range medium, whereas the modern theatre brings its audience into closer contact with the performance. The spectators can see more, and do not need to be told as much; many of the Greek dramatist's techniques are thereby rendered redundant. The measure of this difference can best be judged by comparing a scene in any Greek tragedy with its equivalent from any modern play on the same theme. It should at once be apparent that, where the Greek must use words, the modern can rely heavily on stage directions. What the Greek must take a sentence to say can be conveyed in the modern theatre by a change of facial expression. For these reasons, it has often been suggested that the ideal medium for recreating Greek tragedy in our own time is not the live stage, but radio. Here the audience is once more placed in the Greek position, forced to rely on its ears and its imagination. The most common criticism of Greek tragedy today—at least on the popular level—is that it is too wordy; that too much is said for the little that happens. In most live productions this seems true, but it is the fault not of the dramatist but of the radically changed circumstances of stage presentation.

Here the aesthetic advantages of the puppet become obvious. The limitations of the marionette almost exactly equate those of the Greek actor. The marionette too is deprived, by reason of his rigid features, of the nuances of facial expression. He too is confined to a relatively small range of broad and simple gestures. And in the scale of the performance, the Greek actor-audience relationship is almost exactly restored. The spectator watching a marionette play in a modern theatre will see the performers small, as the Greeks saw them. When a Greek play is performed in this medium, the correct balance returns. Emphasis is shifted from visual effect and goes back to the words, where it belongs.

The same arguments apply to Greek comedy. This deals in broad, often gross, caricature, presenting a procession of exaggerated comic types with much opportunity for slapstick and knockabout comedy as well as for exquisite verbal wit. The best plays of Aristophanes are wild fantasy with a serious underlying moral purpose, and the choruses are often composed of non-human characters such as frogs, clouds, or birds. Here the puppet's own capacity for abstracting, caricaturing, and presenting the surreal can be turned to excellent account. The arguments for presenting Greek drama in this medium are so persuasive that it is surprising that the field has not been more fully exploited. Some excellent work has been done; there have been stimulating productions of Aristophanes' *Birds* at the University of Ohio, and of *The Clouds* at the University of Toronto. Tragedy has been largely neglected. I have myself offered Aeschylus' *Agamemnon*, Sophocles' *Oedipus the King*, Euripides' *Medea* and *Cyclops*, and Aristophanes' *Frogs* and *Birds*. Each author presents his own problems. On the whole, the technical demands of such plays are few. There is little or no violent action and the casts are comparatively small. The major problem is the Greek chorus. Some plays which depend on elaborate choral singing and choreography obviously cannot be performed in this medium. In others the chorus can, without detriment to the play, be pared down to a manageable size. This is particularly true of Euripides, who in his tragedies is often impatient of the old conventions and emphasizes his actors at the expense of his chorus, to the point where the latter becomes virtually redundant. In my production of *Medea*, I reduced the chorus of Corinthian women to two, with the Nurse also serving as a chorus member after her introductory scenes. In *Oedipus the King*, I did not show the chorus at all, but tried to convey its function as observer and commentator by delivering its verses out of the darkness, above an empty stage. This treatment of the chorus as a disembodied, critical voice was in fact right, though right only for this play.

Later Greek and Roman plays developed the comedy of masks to a point where the actors were as rigorously stereotyped as Punch and Judy. Actors wore masks which fitted them at once into familiar and easily identifiable categories, each with its appropriate form of behavior—the angry old man always going about threatening to punish his son, the cunning slave scheming to thwart him, the young lovers, the parasite or social hanger-on. Most of the later Greek plays have perished, but the puppeteer seeking a comedy which combines suitability with literary merit will find in the works of the Roman Plautus and Terence a wealth of material as funny today as when it was first written, and available in a number of excellent translations.

Turning to the English dramatic heritage, the puppeteer will surely find inspiration in the medieval drama. These early plays of the Catholic Church recounted the story of the Bible in terms which the humblest spectator could understand, and in a verse form all the more moving for its simplicity. Short episodes cover most of the Old and New Testaments, from the Creation to the Redemption and beyond. These can be, and have been, performed by marionettes with perfect dignity and reverence. The plays also offer many comic opportunities. An example is the play of the Flood, where Noah argues in vain with his shrewish wife and forces her to board the ark only by giving her a sound beating. Devils in various forms were a regular feature of these plays, and the puppeteer will enjoy reproducing their fantastic masks and costumes, examples of which are still extant.

The later medieval Moralities work through allegory to convey the Christian message. In most cases their characters are completely depersonalized, and represent various bodily or spiritual qualities. In the most famous and most familiar of these plays, *Everyman*, the eponymous protagonist, who represents sinful mankind, is summoned by Death to prepare his account for the Last Judgment. He makes the round of his earthly friends, Good Fellowship, Kindred, Cousin, and Wordly Goods, each of whom, with mounting acrimony, rejects him. He is thus thrown back on his spiritual qualities—Good Deeds, Knowledge, Discretion, and the rest—and, with their help, makes his pilgrimage to the grave and ultimate resurrection. In the puppet medium it is possible to depersonalize the story more completely, and more effectively, than on the live stage, for it is no longer necessary to rely solely on the human form. In my marionette production of *Everyman*, Worldly Goods was represented not as a person but as a massive ironbound chest which slowly opened when Goods was required to speak, and shut with a bang at the close of the scene, when Goods mocks Everyman's appeal for aid and bids him an abrupt adieu. This offered a vivid and effective visual image; Everyman was left kneeling in desperation before an insensate lump of wood and iron.

In the Elizabethan theatre the late Greek and Roman type-comedy, with its rigidly demarcated characters, was taken up by Ben Jonson. He introduced his theory of "humours," according to which an individual's eccentricity was determined by some internal imbalance. Jonson created a gallery of comic types, each distorted in one particular direction. As in the case of the Roman stereotypes, the puppet can aid here by offering visual equivalents to these psychological aberrations. A case in point is Jonson's *Volpone*, a satirical comedy on the folly of human greed set in Renaissance Venice. The central character, Volpone, is a man already rich who steadily increases his wealth by feigning imminent death and accepting gifts from those who hope to become his heirs. In this play the characters' names are all meaningful. "Volpone" means "the fox," the schemer. His servant, Mosca, is "the fly," bustling and parasitical. The citizens who vie for Volpone's favors are various types of predator—Voltore "the vulture," Corbaccio "the raven," Corvino "the crow." One of the most exciting productions of this play that I have seen was in England at the Stratford-on-Avon Festival. Here the suggestion of animality in the names was exploited in the costumes and make-up. Volpone looked like a fox; he wore a red beard and bushy cap, and in the trimmings of his robe there was even the suggestion of a tail. Corbaccio wore rusty black. Even the judges in the culminating trial scene were costumed like owls. In the marionette theatre this idea could be taken even further, and would be perfectly in keeping with Jonson's intentions. The very concept of the "humour" is ideally suited to puppetry.

Nearer our own age, Victorian melodrama recalls Roman comedy in its rigorous system of type-casting; plays were built around the stock figures of the heavy villain, romantic hero, aged father, and innocent heroine. Many of these plays are well worth reviving, and for all their bombast and exaggeration contain excellent dramatic writing. *Maria Marten*, which John Wright has presented so successfully with his marionettes, and *Sweeney Todd, the Demon Barber of Fleet Street*, are well-loved English examples; the contemporary American theatre provided many more.

These are only a few of the fields which the puppeteer can explore for his pleasure and benefit. Other periods of special interest will be discussed elsewhere in the book—the Commedia dell'Arte on pages 93-94, French neoclassical tragedy on page 143. All of them offer excellent plots and fine writing, and subjects which marionettes are, by their nature, well suited to perform. The material will stimulate the puppeteer's powers of invention, and both he and his audience will derive a deeper satisfaction than that which comes from the usual run of puppet plays.

The live drama, then, has much to offer the adventurous and creative puppeteer in search of worthy material. I have also endeavored to suggest in the foregoing pages some of the qualities that puppetry, in its turn, has to offer the live theatre. This is the true test of its claim to be considered as an art form in its own right. To justify their existence puppets must add something of their own to the plays they interpret—some desirable quality which the live theatre is unable to achieve. We have the right to demand of any art that it should contribute something of its own, and not merely repeat what has already been accomplished satisfactorily by another. When a play is transferred to the cinema screen, we require the result to be something more than a pictorial record of the stage performance. We ask that it should add to the drama those peculiarly cinematic qualities—fluidity, range of action, the heightened concentration attainable by close-up—impossible in the live theatre and achieved only by the techniques and resources of the camera. When a novel is dramatized we ask that the play should bring out some aspect of the original conception which the novel form cannot; otherwise, it might as well have remained a novel; the work is sterile and pointless, and has the same relationship to the original that a waxwork has to the living figure, clever, often impressive, but artistically negligible. And in discussing puppet versions of live plays we must ask, similarly, if they add anything, or say anything that has not been said equally well before. If not, Dr. Johnson's dictum on women preachers must apply: the question is not whether it is well or ill done, but why it should be done at all.

There are many ways in which the puppet can contribute. Some of these I have already suggested; in the case of the Greek theatre I have argued that the use of marionettes instead of live actors solves an important historical problem. Several of these uses have already been recognized by workers in the live theatre. Most important is the puppet's power, deriving from its own simplicity, of stripping away inessentials and leading the spectator to the very heart of the drama. The besetting problem of those who would create a work of art in the theatre is unity. Every great work of art presupposes a unity of conception from the original creative impulse to the finished work, modified subtly in the process of creation but substantially the same from beginning to end. It follows naturally that this unity is easiest to achieve when only one creative mind is involved. We see this in the relationship of the artist to his canvas, the sculptor to his stone. In the theatre this unity is likely to be disrupted by the multitude of interpreters. Here we no longer have a simple relationship between the artist and his material but one much more complex, in which author, director, designer, and actors form a large committee where everyone has his own views to put forward. It is no wonder that in attempting to reconcile these views the unity of conception is often lost.

Only very early and very late in theatre history has this danger been minimized. In the Greek theatre the poet was originally his own actor, director, composer, and choreographer, thus retaining control over every aspect of the production in his own hands. Our own time has seen the emergence of the director as the dominating personality, whose function is to weld the contributing talents into a harmonious and coherent whole. Between Euripides and Wagner there was little attempt to see the production as a unity, in which every aspect must be subordinated to the main theme. Even today the director's function is often abused. The director who can resist the temptation to subjugate the author's personality to his own, and to offer a production that reflects himself rather than the play, is lamentably rare.

This fundamental problem has become apparent to several theorists. They have seen the individual personalities of the actors, with the consequent conflict of wills, as intrusive elements in the grand design, and have asked whether the director's relationship to his play could not become as simple as in the other arts. Arthur Symons, writing at the end of the last century, argued that drama had become corrupted by the actors' preoccupation with technique and analysis, and that puppets would provide a simpler and more poetic medium through which the dramatist could speak. The puppet's limitations would strip away all unnecessary elaboration. In *A Theory of the Stage* he took the extreme viewpoint that the foundation of drama was that part of the action which could be represented in dumbshow, and that puppets would provide the vehicle for reducing that action to its simplest and purest terms. In *An Apology for Puppets*, published in 1897, he again insisted that marionettes were the perfect medium, and that their appeal was not to the childish but to the poetic element in all of us.

In 1906 Gordon Craig took up the cause in his article "The Actor and the Uber-Marionette," first published in his own journal, *The Mask*, and later in book form as part of *On the Art of the Theatre*. Craig begins provocatively with the remark of Eleonora Duse: "To save the Theatre, the Theatre must be destroyed, the actors and actresses must all die of plague." Craig held that the actor could best fulfill his purpose by becoming a sort of super-marionette, to work at the director's command and be molded by him as seemed most appropriate; that he should abnegate his own personality to become an instrument on which the director could play.

Symons and Craig were both practical men, and we cannot suppose that they wished to drive the actor from the stage altogether. In later years Craig indignantly defended himself against the storm his article had aroused, insisting that neither Duse's sentiments nor his own were to be taken literally; what he wanted was an actor "plus fire and minus egotism," who would be more responsive to the demands of the play and less to those of his own nature. Both writers saw that the marionette, by dispensing with human personality, could concentrate the spectator's attention more forcefully on the essential conflict of the drama. Craig writes elsewhere of the sad debasement of the puppet in popular esteem, and hold out hopes for the revival of the art-form; in his years of retirement in Paris, he has turned more and more to marionettes, and away from the live theatre.

It has already been noted that in many plays, some of the greatest in world drama, the actor's individuality was not allowed to intrude. The playwright was master and used the actors as symbols of his thought. In Greek drama the actor, masked, padded, and compelled by the vast size of his theatre to use only the simplest and most obviously expressive gestures, was so depersonalized as to become almost a puppet. In the classical No theatre of Japan the actors are similarly masked, declaim in recitative, and move balletically in stylized pantomime; there is little room for the intrusion of personality here. In the medieval Miracle plays emphasis lay not so much on individual characterization as on the exposition of the Bible's message; the later Moralities spoke through the personification of such qualities as Chastity, Knowledge, Strength, and Good Deeds. Modern dramatists like Eugene O'Neill have returned to the mask again and again. We may say, then, that whenever the actor dons a mask—either literally, as in the Greek and Roman plays, or figuratively, as when playing a strongly typed part—he is abnegating his individuality and making of himself a puppet; and in such cases the marionette may legitimately claim to perform his functions at least as well, and sometimes better.

Here puppets can restore to the production that unity for which the live theatre often seeks in vain. With the actors gone, the number of minds at work is reduced. Most puppet companies consist of only two or three people. Often one man alone designs and works the puppets, paints the scenery, and plans the lighting. Thus the production becomes the director's ideal, an organic whole proceeding from one creative mind with every element given its due importance, rather than the amalgamation of a set of disparate talents which must be coerced into something like harmony. For the poetic play, the drama of imagination and ideas, the artist will find in puppets a well-nigh perfect medium of expression, for with only one mind, or few at most, interposing themselves between the author and the finished work, there is less risk of obscuring the issue with irrelevancies, and the play will benefit in consequence.

# Stage, Setting, and Cast

### THE STAGE

In its essentials, the conventional marionette stage has a family resemblance to its full-size prototype. It consists of three main units: the stage floor, the proscenium, and the elevated "bridge" which serves both to accommodate the operators and as a rear wall on which to mount scenic backdrops. My first stage was designed on these lines, except that the demands of portability have always forced me to dispense with an elaborate bridge. The stage platform was constructed in the form of two large, shallow boxes hinged together. When opened out they offered a sufficiently spacious acting area, and, when closed, a suitcase into which the superstructure could be packed. The proscenium was a light wooden framework attached to the two front corners of the platform, and draped with black fabric; at the rear two uprights and a connecting crossbar provided, if not a bridge, at least a rail on which my arms could rest and to which scenery could be attached.

I used this structure for several years, but grew gradually more dissatisfied with it. The proscenium was a particular annoyance. In the first place it greatly increased the weight I had to carry. In performance it made the projection of the voice a considerable strain, particularly in large halls. The words had to penetrate this expanse of fabric, this large black screen, and this was not always easy. It was also a constricting factor psychologically, if not physically. While operating I was always conscious of the proximity of this front wall, and afraid that I might hit it or tangle the marionette strings on it. These objections caused me to think seriously about the necessity of using a proscenium at all, and in the course of my contemplations I hit upon an idea which has been at the basis of my presentations ever since.

It seemed to me that the structure of the conventional marionette stage embodied precisely the fallacy that in my performances I had been trying to eradicate—the idea that the function of puppetry was simply to present live entertainment in miniature, that the marionette, by virtue of ingenious mechanics and manipulation, should approximate as closely as possible a scaled-down human being, and that the audience should be convinced that the marionettes, Pinocchio-like, lived a life of their own and were not controlled by any other agency. Once one accepts this view of puppetry, it follows inevitably that the proscenium is seen as necessary and natural, for the operators must be concealed at all costs. Even the strings must be hidden as best they can. Some puppeteers have gone to great lengths to attain this end, using superfine thread or painting their strings to merge with the scenery.

As I have tried to convey in the foregoing chapters, I have never been interested in puppets in this limited, representational sense; rather, I was concerned to exploit them as a formal device for stressing certain dramatic values. Why, then, use a proscenium? Did it, in fact, matter so much if the operator was revealed? I found myself becoming more and more interested in presentational methods of puppetry, for which there is both ancient and modern precedent.

The traditional puppet theatre of Japan has customarily allowed its operators to be seen. Here the puppets are large, far larger than most European or American figures; they are controlled by rods, and brightly dressed. The operator, although in full view, wears black. Though always visible, he is never obtrusive. The attention of the audience is focused on the moving figures, but the distinction between illusion and reality is kept perfectly clear. These Japanese puppets, in fact, achieve an "alienation effect" akin to that for which Brecht has striven on the live stage. (Brecht, incidentally, would make intriguing material for puppets.) It is a device that removes at one blow the childishness and pseudo-sentimentality liable to attach itself to Western puppet performers. American and English reviewers, when they notice the puppet stage at all, tend to regress to the nursery for their descriptive phrases and parade such nauseous appellations as "little people" or "moppet actors." It would be unthinkable to apply these terms, or the attitude which produces them, to a Japanese performance. The audience sees the puppet as an instrument on which the operator plays to achieve certain sorts of effect, as a violinist plays upon his violin, and the open admission of artifice is not detrimental to the performance but rather the reverse.

Western operators have also used the open-stage method, but usually for night-club or cabaret performances where the exigencies of staging prevent the erection of a full theatre. Some employ a simple curtain as a background, others operate their figures in a spotlight only, with no scenic backing at all. These practices have usually, however, been considered as proper to this specialized type of performance only, and for this reason have had less effect on the popular view of puppet staging than they should have had.

Together, these ideas led me to abolish the proscenium. The first experiment was made for a production of Aristophanes' *The Frogs*. I felt that here I had the justification that the play was written for an open and not a proscenium stage, so that to present the audience with an unimpeded view of the platform would at least have an excuse in theatre history. The gain in diction and the feeling of freedom were so striking that I have never returned to the proscenium since. The loss of that concentration of effect which the proscenium can give is more than made up by the gain in intimacy, the feeling of direct rapport with the audience, without the interference of a physical barrier. Nor am I convinced that there is, in fact, any such loss of concentration large enough to be significant.

My present stage has been reduced to two simple units, the stage floor and the back screen. This screen is shown in position in plate 2; the stage floor is omitted to make the details of construction clearer. It will be apparent that the upper half of my body is not concealed. In performance, I follow the practice of the Japanese operators in wearing a black shirt, and black gloves with the thumb and forefinger removed to facilitate operation. Thus, as in the Japanese shows, the operator's presence is felt, but is not obtrusive. Lighting is focused on the stage, and the operator is left in darkness. I have found that after the first few seconds the audience is oblivious to my presence and concentrates wholly on the marionette action. The convention of my "invisibility" is easily created and easily accepted. Even when I have been compelled to perform in halls less than adequately darkened, and was in full view of anyone who cared to see, I have found that the audience preferred to concentrate on the play and not on the manipulation.

This opening up of the stage created a number of side effects which were at first accidental, and have since been turned to use in production. The shadows cast by the puppets on the walls of the hall can occasionally be turned to dramatic account. In *Doctor Faustus* I have used low-level sidelighting on the figure of Mephistopheles in his first dialogue with Faustus to give the effect of a small, brightly lit figure on the stage dwarfed by a huge shadow on the wall. It is also possible to utilize the presence of the operator, drawing attention to him by direct or reflected illumination, for certain sorts of scene. The sudden contrast between the marionette and this apparent giant can be very exciting, as I shall suggest in Chapter Four.

The back screen, as in the illustration, is draped in black. For some plays backdrops are hung in front of this, for others it serves by itself as the backdrop, in combination with built-up scenic units placed on the main stage. A chain running along the top of the screen on the reverse side holds the marionettes waiting for their entrance. A chain is used, in preference to a cord, so that the marionettes will not slide towards the center and tangle with each other. Two swinging arms mounted on the front of the screen (see plate 2) hold puppets that are on stage but at rest. These arms cover most of the acting area, and make it possible for a single operator to control even a large cast.

The stage floor itself is hinged for easy transportation; in performance, it is braced by light aluminum trestles which give approximately seven inches of understage space. This floor is pierced by a large trapdoor, primarily for use in Elizabethan plays. I have used it for the hellish appearances in *Doctor Faustus*, for Volpone's treasure chest in *Volpone*, and for several scenes in *Everyman*. In the latter play, it is from the trap that Death arises when he is first summoned by God; it is from here that Good Deeds first appears ("Here I lie, cold in the ground . . . .") and, of course, it represents the grave into which Everyman descends at the end of the play. Like the marionettes themselves, its operation has to be controlled from above by a string. This method is not ideal, and in a theatre erected on a permanent site it would probably be better to have it controlled from below by a foot-pedal—the fewer strings the better.

#### THE SETTING

The live-stage designer has a large amount of space to fill. Besides providing the units necessary for the action, he must

contrive to fill this space with something that is both appropriate and visually interesting, so that if the spectator's eye
wanders from the actors it will always find something meaningful and attractive. In the marionette theatre the spectator's
eye cannot wander very far. Here the designer has only a limited space to make his statement; he must be concise where
the live-stage designer can afford to be expansive. He must
also bear in mind that no detail will carry very far. This is one
of the greatest dangers in creating settings for this medium.
Construction is so much easier than on the live stage. It is
possible to create, for example, the most elaborate baroque
set with the minimum of labor and with materials that may be
picked up anywhere; but in practice, little more than the
broad outlines will be seen beyond the first few rows.

If the set is to assist the play and not obscure it, it must use
the fewest possible units, the simplest lines, and the minimum
of decoration. For these reasons the best suggestions for design will often come, not from live theatre practice, but from
display advertising and kindred arts. A store-window display
is not designed for the leisured contemplation of an audience
that has assembled for the express purpose of watching it.
It must make a strong and immediate impact on the casual
passer-by, who probably has his mind on other things; and if
it conveys its initial message forcefully enough, it will stop
him in his tracks and make him return for a second look.
Similarly, the puppet stage design must make an immediate
and vivid impact, even on the spectator at the back of the
hall. It must use the same economy of expression. Although
live-stage practice should by no means be neglected—designs
for the ballet are particularly useful—the occasional half-hour
spent studying the windows of Marshall Field or Lord and
Taylor will probably be more beneficial.

In my own theatre, the use of the open stage has dictated
further limitations. Settings cannot be changed except in a
blackout or by some mechanical means; the sudden appearance of a huge hand to shift scenery would strain the conven-

tion too far. But blackout changes are dangerous, and mechanical devices hardly less so. I have usually had to fall back on a permanent set, which could serve with only minor modifications for all the locations required in the play; and in this I have been assisted by the fact that the plays I perform—Greek, Roman, Elizabethan, and French—were intended for this sort of setting in their original representation, and their texts were composed with these problems in mind. Experiment has shown that some modification of the original setting gives the flexibility that is needed.

Quite apart from the practical advantages, I find it useful and important to give audiences—particularly student audiences, with whom I am mostly concerned—a historical view of the play by putting it into an approximation of its original setting. Thus, for the Greek plays, I have usually employed the basic features of the fifth-century Athenian theatre, reduced to their simplest terms—a simple architectural façade, doors, an altar. This basic plan can be simplified or expanded in various ways, depending on the demands of the particular work, and the elements rearranged in different combinations. For Aeschylus' *Agamemnon*, the set was dominated by a pair of doors, several times larger than the marionettes, which represented the entrance to Agamemnon's palace. These doors were ornamented with a Gorgon's head. At the end of the tragedy, when Agamemnon has been murdered and his wife and her lover have assumed authority in the city, the stage lights slowly dimmed until nothing was visible but this head, lit by a solitary spotlight. In *Oedipus the King*, I felt it necessary to increase the visual interest by employing as many different levels as possible. The architectural background was retained, a central altar gave a focus-point, and ramps led from stage to ground level at the front of the stage and at each side (see plates 11, 12). This made more varied entrances possible —characters appeared at ground level, and made their way up the ramps to the stage—and suggested several interesting lighting effects. It was often possible to hold a minor character in semi-silhouette on the ramp while a more important character moved in full light on the stage above him.

A more complicated setting was used for the medieval *Everyman*. We have no evidence for the original staging of this play, though all the indications suggest that it was performed against a series of mansions—scenic units representing the various locations required—which were arranged before the audience in simultaneous view. The actors would have moved from one mansion to another as the action dictated, and those mansions not in immediate use would have been, by convention, ignored. In this play above all I felt the need for some scenic elaboration. *Everyman*, although a very exciting and complex work, can easily become tedious on the stage. It is written largely in the form of a series of conversations between Everyman and the various personified aspects of his life to whom he turns for help in his last hours on earth. The action may be summarized as follows:

1. God announces His dissatisfaction with mankind, and His intention of calling Everyman to make his final reckoning.
2. God summons Death and orders him to announce to Everyman that he must prepare his account with all speed.
3. Death accosts Everyman, tells him that his last hour is come, and orders him to present himself, with his reckoning, before God without delay.
4. Everyman, in despair, seeks for someone to accompany him on this dreadful journey. He asks Good Fellowship, who rejects him.
5. He asks Kindred and Cousin, who similarly reject him.
6. He asks Worldly Goods, who not only rejects him but announces that his function is to destroy men's souls.
7. Everyman turns to Good Deeds, who is too weak from neglect to accompany him. She suggests, however, that

he go with Knowledge to the house of Confession, and there make amends for his past sins.

8. Everyman visits Confession and undergoes penance. Good Deeds, reinvigorated, comes to join him and Knowledge.

9. Together they call on the qualities that Everyman must take with him to the grave—Strength, Beauty, Discretion, and Five-Wits.

10. They arrive at the grave. One by one, all Everyman's qualities leave him except for Good Deeds, who will accompany him before the throne of God.

11. Everyman descends into the grave. An angel announces that he has been cleansed of his sins, and may ascend to join the blessed in Heaven.

It seemed important here to provide as varied a pattern of action as possible, in order that this series of dialogues should not seem static or repetitive, and at the same time to offer a shifting setting which would underscore the theme and dynamics of the play. The medieval plan was used as the basis. Two mansions were located at opposite sides of the stage. One represented the World, the other the Church. These were hinged to the stage floor, and collapsible; when not required, they would fold down flush with the floor level and would not be seen. When needed, a string could pull them upright into position. The stage floor already had its trap, virtually a third mansion which could be used for the grave and for the first appearance of Good Deeds, as already described.

The staging of God's speech, and His dialogue with Death, presented a number of problems. Some means had to be found of representing the presence of the Deity strikingly and powerfully without giving offense. In medieval performances the presence of God on the stage was considered natural and proper; a satisfactory distinction between Him and the other characters could be achieved visually or orally. In some plays

God wore a gold mask, and in one French presentation His voice was represented by four speakers, each with a different vocal range, speaking in unison to give an effect more power-ful, and more unearthly, than any single voice could have achieved. I sought for some device of this nature that would open the play on the right note. For some time I considered having no visible indication of God's presence at all, but play-ing the whole scene in darkness and relying on voice alone; then, of tape-recording God's speech to give it a different vocal quality from those of the other speakers, whose words would be read live. This idea was in the end rejected, chiefly because the speech is such a long one that the audience needs some visual focus if interest is to be maintained to the end. There is a limit to the length of time that audiences will listen to speeches in the dark.

I finally hit on a solution that made use of the contrast be-tween the size of the operator and the scale of the puppet theatre, a device to which I have referred earlier. This sort of effect is very easy to obtain with the open-stage method. At the beginning of the play, the stage was completely empty. The two mansions were folded down out of sight and the grave-trap was closed; there was nothing to see but the black rear curtain. The presence of God was signified by my own hand, gloveless, and working through a slit cut halfway up the backcloth. It was lit by a single red spotlight, and, in this position, gave the effect of a gigantic hand poised over the scene of the coming action. This device was simple, and still impressive. The speech supplies hints for a number of signifi-cant gestures—the hand turning slowly, with the fingers out-stretched as if in agony, when God describes the suffering on the Cross; the hand flattening and making a thrusting motion towards the ground, when He talks of visiting His wrath on mankind; a single stabbing forefinger to indicate the where-abouts of Death. The device of the hand of God pointing from the heavens is, of course, frequent in medieval illustrations;

here was an effect which at the same time gave interest to the speech and was stylistically appropriate to its period. When Death finally emerged from the trap, the contrast between this small skeletonic figure and the apparently huge hand of God was startling.

When Death had received his instructions, and turned to accost Everyman, the "World" mansion was raised, and all the scenes between the protagonist and his earthly associates —Fellowship, Kindred, Cousin, and Worldly Goods—were played in front of it. Only the small area around the mansion was lit, so that characters entered out of the darkness, played their short scenes, and vanished into the darkness again. As described in Chapter Two, the character of Worldly Goods was portrayed not by a human figure but by a large chest that opened and shut. When Goods finally rejected Everyman, and he realized that he could find no help or comfort among his mortal companions, the "World" mansion descended rapidly and with a loud noise—the collapse of Everyman's material aspirations—leaving him to soliloquize, alone and desolate, on a stage black and empty as it had been when the play opened.

The following sequences took the action to the other side of the stage. When Good Deeds appeared from the trap and directed Everyman to go with Knowledge to Confession, the "Church" mansion was raised. Everyman's appeal to Confession, his invocation of his various attributes, and his subsequent conversations with them took place in this location. When the companions started on their last journey to the grave, the "Church" mansion was lowered, leaving the stage once again empty.

The last scene, where Everyman bids farewell to his Strength, Beauty, and other attributes, was located at centerstage above the grave-trap itself. At the moment of death, Everyman descended into the grave, and the trap slowly closed upon him. This is the moment, curiously enough, at which many live productions choose to end the play. Although the voice of the Angel promises resurrection, Everyman is allowed to remain in his tomb. It seemed to me that, if the play was to have its full effect, Everyman must be seen again, and his reemergence must be accompanied by some *coup de théâtre*, some device more vivid and striking than any that had been used before. Therefore, at the moment of resurrection, the black drape, which until now had masked the rear of the stage, rose to reveal an elaborate stained glass window that covered the whole area. It was lit from behind, and there was no front lighting at all save for a single spotlight on Everyman. Although this effect lasted scarcely half a minute, it offered a satisfactory climax; the darkness of the earlier scenes had been replaced by light, and Everyman ascended into Heaven.

I have discussed *Everyman* in such detail and at such length because it shows, perhaps more clearly than any of my other productions, the extent to which it is necessary both to free oneself from live-theatre preconceptions and to reappraise the traditional criteria of the marionette stage. In this version, the customary distinctions between puppet, setting, and operator were abolished. Could one say precisely what was a puppet and what was not? In the case of the speech by God, the human hand, unadorned, was used as a puppet. In the later sequences, the stage settings were used virtually as puppets, controlled by the same means and responding to the movements and the mood of the stage action. Throughout the play the use of selective lighting, and the isolation of scenic units against a dark background, gave the effect of a black void shot through with occasional strands of bright color; and this, in itself, is a not ineffective image to convey the medieval state of mind.

### THE LIGHTING

In lighting the marionette stage, as in designing settings for it, the limitation of size must be kept constantly in mind. In the live theatre the lighting designer has a large area at his disposal and can light various portions of this selectively as the action demands. In marionette work, one begins with the necessity of demarcating a small area in a large hall, and, because of this, one is often compelled to avoid subtlety and delicacy of effect and be content with allowing the lighting to fulfill its primary function, that of illuminating the action. There are also a number of technical difficulties in the sensitive control of small-scale lighting, and, particularly in the case of a theatre which must travel, the equipment needed takes up more room than it is worth. Thus the marionette operator must normally content himself with fewer light-sources, and less flexible control of color, direction, and strength, than are possible in the live theatre.

My own lighting equipment is extremely simple. Two permanent standards, mounted at the front corners of the stage, carry four floods for general illumination. These make it possible to light each side of the stage independently. There are a number of additional lamps which can be placed about the stage as required, usually concealed behind scenic units, to give more light where it is needed or for special effects. The use of the open stage rules out the possibility of footlighting except where it is desirable that the operator should be seen. These lamps are controlled by a small eight-circuit switchboard mounted on the rear of the stage and convenient to the hand. I originally used transformer voltages, with small rheostats as dimmers, but have more recently operated directly from the main supply, with on-off switches only and no dimming. This measure was forced on me by the ever-present problem of weight, but my present system, although I am no longer able to control intensity, gives a stark effect which has its own virtues.

With this type of lighting, as in so many aspects of marionette theatre, it is necessary to depart substantially from live theatre practice. In live theatre, blocking dictates lighting. The director positions and moves his actors as he wants them, and the lighting engineer then adjusts his instruments so that the illumination follows them in performance. In marionette theatre the reverse tends to be true. Light sources are fewer and fixed; position, angle, and color can only rarely be changed during the course of the performance. Thus it is often necessary for the lighting to dictate the blocking. Imagine, for example, a dialogue between two characters in which it is desired to bring first one and then the other into prominence. This can be accomplished by lighting from a single source, and moving each character in turn into the lighted area—or, alternatively, by positioning one character between his partner and the light-source, casting a shadow on him and leaving him in obscurity, until it is desirable that he should be brought into prominence. Then the first character moves away and the second leaps into plain view.

Several interesting effects can be secured by moving the marionette in relation to the light rather than vice versa. I hit on one for *Oedipus the King*, in the scene where Oedipus calls down a curse on the unknown murderer of Laius. Oedipus delivered most of this speech standing behind the altar which occupied center stage (see plate 12). This altar was hollow, and in it was concealed a small light, barely two inches away from Oedipus, so that it lit him alone, from below, and cast interesting shadows on the modelling of his face. There was no other light on the stage. By moving Oedipus slightly backward and forward as he spoke, and shifting him in relation to the path of the light, it was possible to create a suggestion of flickering flames from the altar playing on his face and robes. In live stage practice it would have been the light, here it was the puppet, that flickered, but the effect was the same.

## THE MARIONETTES

The construction of my marionettes does not differ from customary practice except in the controls and stringing, which are discussed separately below. Over the years I have used wooden bodies, cloth bodies, and a combination of the two; on the whole I am inclined to favor bodies made completely of cloth, both because of the saving in weight and for the opportunities they offer in costuming. For historical periods involving skin-tight costumes, such as those worn by some of the Commedia dell'Arte figures, it is neater and more convenient to make the limbs in appropriately colored cloth from the beginning, or to paint directly onto the fabric of the body, rather than to use a costume proper. This makes for greater ease of movement and gives a better impression of slimness and elegance.

But bodies are more or less the same for all figures. It is in the head and hands that character lies, and here the puppeteer has his greatest advantage over the live theatre: he can style his characters in the same way that he styles his set. It is good to be able to create characters to order. This is an advantage which reveals itself perhaps most obviously in puppet productions of opera. In live production it is often necessary to sacrifice looks to vocal quality; the singer whose voice is right for the role is not always suitable in appearance. We are all familiar with the large ladies who sing exquisitely, but fail to convince us that they are dying of consumption. When puppets perform to a recorded score, their physical presence can be as exquisite as their voices. There are few live opera heroines more fetching, or more ethereal, than the Salzburg Marionette Theatre's Queen of Night, or the Kungsholm Gilda. This may seem a frivolous example; but opera is a conspicuous example of a type of theatre where the creator's ideal can rarely be realized in performance, and puppets offer one solution to this dilemma. Some operatic films have used a basically similar method, with personable mimes synchronizing their lips to a prerecorded sound track; this is no more than an extension, in purely human terms, of the same idea.

In the case of the serious drama, the puppeteer may adapt the pictorial conventions of the appropriate period to his characters as well as to his scenery. Often the original staging of the plays will suggest a convention which may be easily adapted to the new medium. Mask plays are an obvious example. Greek and Roman plays, the Japanese No drama, and the Commedia dell'Arte were all written to be played in masks, and there is usually pictorial evidence, if the masks themselves are not extant, that the puppeteer can copy for his own purposes. In my performances of Greek and Roman plays I have always used the mask-types as appropriate (see plates 2-7, 10-12); it is yet another way in which the marionette stage can aid in bringing to life the play that the original audience knew, both in its sound and in its appearance.

Although we have little detailed information about the Greek masks, we can at least reconstruct them in outline. With the Commedia dell'Arte we are more fortunate. Contemporary illustrations, and sometimes actual surviving masks, show us exactly how each of the stock characters looked during the time in which the Commedia flourished. I have used this convention of masks in a production of *Les Fourberies de Scapin*, by Molière. The Italian popular comedy had considerable influence on the seventeenth-century French stage, and on Molière in particular. In his early touring days he came into contact with leading Commedia players who were working in provincial France at this time, and their influence was to remain with him all his life. He uses the stock characters of the Commedia in several of his shorter plays—sometimes under French names—and often employs what seems to be traditional Italian stage business.

Although written toward the end of Molière's career, in 1671, *Les Fourberies de Scapin* has strong affinities with the Commedia. It is a tale, based on the Latin of Terence, of two young men who find themselves in amorous difficulties. One has married a destitute girl, apparently without family or fortune, and the other, in love with a young gypsy, lacks the money to buy her from her masters. Their problems are solved, and the boys reconciled with their fathers, by the agency of their servant and go-between Scapin, a master of ingenious plots and devices. The principal characters are drawn directly from the Commedia, some with virtually the same names. Scapin himself is a French version of the Italian Scapino; the two fathers, one miserly and the other pompous and overbearing, recall the Italian Pantalone and the Doctor; the straight parts, the two rather colorless young men and their inamoratas, are also modelled directly on Italian proto-types. It thus seemed perfectly justifiable to present this comedy as a Commedia production, as it often is on the live stage, and use the traditional masks and costumes (see plates 13-20).

My aim here was to exploit the Commedia idea that the mask is the character, and that the wearing of this mask imposes on the individual performer a preordained line of comic business and a stereotyped mode of behavior. Thus the basic heads for all characters in the play were identical—egg-shapes, featureless, and indistinguishable from one another. Over these were superimposed the various forms of the mask—the black half-mask of the Doctor (see plate 15), the wrinkled brown leather of Pantalone (see plate 16), the grotesque and distorted features of the comic servants (see plate 13). The heads in themselves were nothing; it was only the mask that gave individuality, and in each case the eyes were deliberately left blank and hollow to show that these were only masks, the shell of a character with nothing inside. Even with the mask-less characters the same rule obtained. On the young men and their girls, the features were not modelled, but simply painted onto the surface with as few lines as possible (see plates 14, 18, 19).

For maskless drama, other conventions will readily suggest themselves. The characters for *Everyman* were modelled after medieval woodcarvings, broad in conception and execution and limited to the medieval range of colors. Even in plays that demand more realistic treatment, for example in Racine (see plates 8, 9), I like to leave faces comparatively rough and unfinished. As I have suggested earlier, too polished a finish or too detailed an execution leaves no room for the imagination to work. As long as the features are sketched in, and the carving or modelling is sufficiently deep to allow for the play of shadows, the audience will often believe that they see the expression demanded by the words and action of the moment, and what is more, see that expression change before their eyes. This is as true for puppets as it is for full-size masks. Anyone who has worked with masks knows that in performance they are not rigid or impassive; rather, they form a blank screen on which the audience may project the emotions that the words suggest to them; and for this reason, in modelling, it is safer to put in too little than too much.

### STRINGS AND CONTROLS

My marionettes use the standard number of nine strings, which are adequate for the normal range of movements—one to each shoulder, supporting the weight of the figure; one to each side of the head (though this is usually a single string, running through a screw-eye in the control bar, and thus making a considerable range of head-movements possible with the use of one finger only); one to each hand; one to each knee; and one to the small of the back. Some figures have more, some considerably less. There is no point in making complications by stringing a figure for a movement that the play will never require it to perform. I have found it helpful to string the head slightly more loosely than is customary, so that it tilts downward. By applying one finger to the head-string and taking up the slack, small movements can be imparted to the head which are useful in conversations.

For the presentation of full-length plays I have found it necessary to make certain changes in the traditional control. After working for some time with the two normal types, the vertical and the horizontal, I found that they took up too much space for my purposes. It was frequently necessary to bring two characters, or whole groups of characters, into close contact on the stage—particularly in the case of a Greek chorus—and on these occasions there was always the danger that the controls would mesh. I was faced with the problem of reducing the controlling mechanism to as small a compass as possible, with a minimum of projecting pieces. After some experiment, I evolved the simple form seen in plate 1. It consists of one bar only, four or five inches long for a marionette eighteen inches to two feet in height. The arm strings are mounted at each end. Next, working from the ends inward, come the shoulder strings, and in the center the run-through string for the head. Two nails or wires project forward to carry the leg-strings, and a screw eye behind for the back string. A hook mounted on top allows the control to be hung. This type of control will present initial difficulties to those accustomed to larger mechanisms, but has several distinct advantages—not least, the fact that at a pinch it can be held and manipulated in one hand. The puppet's hand-strings are held to the control by thumbtacks; these can easily be taken off, and make it easier to sort out tangles. So can the screw eyes on which most of the other strings are mounted.

### MANIPULATION, DELIVERY, AND PERFORMANCE

From the very beginning of my work, although I have occasionally used others as stage-hands or readers, I have clung to the idea of one-man performance. Mechanically, this is much easier than it looks and sounds. Given the right choice of play, and enough ways of suspending figures who are on stage but not engaged in the immediate action, there are few problems. The plays I have performed have usually been those involving, like Greek or French tragedy, small casts and a minimum of violent action, or those in which, although the casts are larger, the action involves one central character with a number of minor figures who appear only for short times. Marlowe's *Doctor Faustus* and Aristophanes' *The Birds* are examples of this type. I have always felt the need to carry through into the performance the unity of conception that I have been able to give to the design of the play, and have found, in practice, that this unity could best be achieved by controlling all the manipulation myself. This is a procedure that will have no appeal for some. For educators who see the production of a marionette play as an ideal group project calling on the skills and imagination of a whole community, it will obviously be out of the question. For me, the marionette stage is an instrument on which I may play, the extension and diversification of my own personality as an actor. It is a way of combining the intensity and simplicity that a solo reading may give, stripping the play down to its bare essentials, with some of the visual qualities of a full production: of giving full weight to the words of the poet-dramatist, while offering enough stage action to make those words completely meaningful.

There are problems, and there are advantages. In the case of mechanical difficulty, although another pair of hands would be useful in setting things to rights, it is far easier to maintain continuity when only one operator is employed. Individual reaction times vary, and it is not always possible to communicate to a partner, in the course of performance, what the nature of the difficulty is until it is too late; and by this time the audience is conscious that all is not as it should be. I have found one-man operation particularly useful in the problem of synchronizing puppet movement with the lines of the play. This question of synchronization is all-important, and it seems to me that however many operators there are, each operator should speak his own figure's part. Most marionette theatres use additional readers who have no physical contact with the marionette, although they observe its movement from the wings. It is rarely possible, except with a team who have worked together for so long and know each other so well that they can virtually read each other's minds, for perfect synchronization to be achieved in this way.

Recordings are different. In opera production—except in the case of small chamber operas—it is usually necessary to use them. But with a recording the timing and inflections are fixed and can be memorized. The sound of the performance will be exactly the same on each occasion, and the operator can, with sufficient rehearsal, adapt himself to this. The production of marionette opera is, in many ways, an invaluable technical exercise. A live reading can adjust itself to any mechanical difficulty. However well rehearsed one is, there are a thousand and one things that may go wrong at any performance. If the strings snarl, or a light fails, it is usually possible to improvise and cover up the incident. I have found in practice that audiences tend not to notice mechanical failures unless they are blatant or there is some obviously unpremeditated pause in the action; they are uncannily skillful in distinguishing between a pause that has been rehearsed and one that has not. But with recorded sound, the words and music go grinding remorselessly on, and the operator has to extricate himself from his difficulties as quickly as he can or the whole scene may be ruined.

I am not in favor of using recorded dialogue for plays. In comedy, audience responses vary so much from place to place, and from one social situation to another, that it is impossible to predict how long the laughs will be and where they will come, and to make allowances for this in the recording. This is a difficulty, of course, that film has to contend with; it is a profitable exercise to watch the same film comedy in different parts of the country and see how in each place some part, but a different part, of the dialogue is lost in laughter. In tragedy the same problem does not exist, but even here the sense of immediacy is lost by the use of recordings. It is diffi-

cult to establish any true sense of communion with the marionette when the sound is coming from one source and the
movement-control from another; and it seems to me important
that the operator should try to identify himself with the marionette as closely as possible, to regard it as an extension of himself and not as a being separate and apart.

With one operator, or with only a few, the available vocal
range is limited, and even the largest marionette theatres can
rarely supply a separate operator or reader for each character.
Thus it is important to make as clear a vocal distinction as
possible between the various characters, and to supplement
this with visual aids as appropriate. There are certain obvious
methods of vocal differentiation that can be used, depending
on the needs of the play. Dialect is one of them. In my original
production of Aristophanes' *The Birds*, in Great Britain, I had
the problem of distinguishing between over twenty characters, and used at least seven regional dialects to help me to do
so. In comedy, particularly Greek comedy, such a device is
useful and appropriate—Aristophanes himself relied heavily
on Greek dialects for some of his comic effects, and it is permissible to parallel these by similar effects in English.

In tragedy it is not so easy to use dialects or speech-man-
nerisms, but neither is the problem so great as it at first appears.
The plays which I have presented, ranging in time from the
fifth century B.C. to the seventeenth century A.D., have had
one feature in common: in each case they were intended, at
their original representation, to be spoken with a formal delivery which did not attempt to reproduce the rhythms,
speech-patterns, and inflections of real life. This seems to
have been particularly true of the Greek plays. They employed
a standardized delivery, deemed appropriate for tragedy,
which varied little from one character to another; kings and
beggars, old men and young, would have delivered their lines
in approximately the same way, and there would have been
little attempt at the quality of vocal impersonation for which

the modern actor strives and which he envisages as a necessary part of his performance. Nor would there even have
been a vocal differentiation between men and women, for
there were no actresses in the Greek theatre—nor in the
Roman, nor in the English theatre until the Restoration. Thus
the use of one voice, or of a few voices, to represent a whole
range of characters, has some historical justification. Here
again the marionette production may be more faithful to the
mood and feeling of the original than a live production can
now be.

What was true for Greek drama was also true, to a lesser
extent, of Elizabethan tragedy—though there is more scholarly dispute over this—and of French neoclassical tragedy.
In the latter case, of course, actresses were used, but even here
the employment of a deliberately artificial style of delivery
would have minimized distinctions between individuals. Playwrights writing for this style of performance normally make
allowances for the problems of identification that it presents.
It will be clear from the reading of any Greek tragedy that
the poets saw the necessity of making it obvious to their audiences, as forcefully and as often as possible, which character
was which. This was for them a visual as well as an aural
problem. Audiences could not be expected to distinguish one
character from another by his voice alone, nor, given the size
of the theatre and the formal nature of the stage costumes,
could they make a rapid visual distinction. Thus the Greek
tragedians are always very careful to tell us who is who. A
character is identified by name on his first appearance, and
reidentified at any point in the play when doubt in the audience's mind could be harmful. Thus the Greek dramatist has
solved many of the puppeteer's problems for him, simply because the two media are, in many ways, so similar.

I have found in performance that only a slight difference
in inflection is necessary to help the audience distinguish between one character and another, provided that the character

speaking is also moving. A gesture, however small, will show to whom the voice belongs, and the audience will readily accept the convention. It is highly probable—though we have no certain evidence for this—that the Greeks used a similar technique themselves; I have found it useful in my own live productions of Greek tragedy in masks. Within the conventions of Greek and Elizabethan drama it is perfectly convincing, as well as historically correct, for a man to speak women's parts. Even in Racine I have found audiences willing to accept a masculine-voiced Phèdre, along with the other conventions of the play; this would not be possible, however, in any drama more naturalistically oriented.

Off-stage voices offer a special problem if this identification of voice with movement is to be preserved. I may illustrate this from the opening scenes of Euripides' *Medea*. The play opens with a soliloquy by Medea's old nurse. She tells of the desperate plight of her mistress since her husband Jason has deserted her, and hints of possible trouble to come. There enter to her the children of Medea and Jason and their tutor. While the latter is conversing with the Nurse, we hear Medea for the first time, though we still do not see her. She is lamenting her ill-fortune inside the house, and her off-stage voice continues to interrupt the Nurse and Tutor and later the chorus of women who have come to sympathize. Medea does not make her entrance until some time afterwards.

Here then is a particular difficulty. The audience must identify this off-stage voice with Medea from the beginning if the lines are to have meaning. But she is not on stage, and in the marionette production the danger exists that the audience may assume, for the first few lines at least, that it is still the Nurse who is speaking. Some way had to be found of making the identification clear from the beginning, and I eventually solved the problem by falling back on a traditional device of puppetry, the shadow play. As ultimately constructed, the set for *Medea* consisted of two simple units—a set of columns to lend variety to entrances and blocking, and a panel representing a portion of Medea's house (see plate 2). This was in fact a small shadow screen. As Medea spoke her off-stage lines, her shadow was projected onto the screen from behind, and gave the audience the visual clue that they needed. Medea was in the scene, but not of it, throughout.

The shadow screen was used again later in the play in a similar situation, the sequence showing the murder of Medea's children by their own mother. Euripides brings the children on early in the play, and they are constantly in view as it progresses. There is a moving scene where Medea pretends to make a reconciliation with Jason, and calls the children to embrace their father. It is here that the audience feels one of its rare moments of sympathy with Jason; it is obvious from the way in which he talks to his young sons that he loves them and wants to see them grow up into fine men, even if his selfishness has blinded him to his obligations toward their mother. It is this love for his children on which Medea trades; by killing them, she can punish Jason more powerfully and terribly than by killing him. Thus the children are vital figures in the play. But they never speak—never, that is, until the moment of their deaths. For most of the play other characters speak to them, or deliver speeches over them, but the children themselves are never heard from, and their silence amid the clamor of their elders has its own pathetic effect. Their deaths occur off-stage, as deaths normally do in Greek tragedy, and it is at this point that we hear their voices for the first time, pleading for protection from their own mother.

This scene raised a problem similar to that discussed earlier. Once again, the audience was presented with the voice of an off-stage character whom they had not yet heard speaking. This was a point in the play where any delay or confusion in identifying the voice would have been disastrous. Once again, the shadow screen offered a solution. As the children cried in terror, the main stage lighting was darkened completely, and only the two shadows were visible. The screen lighting turned to red; Medea's shadow was seen rising behind those of the children, her arm menacingly upraised. As it fell, there was a sudden blackout, a choking gasp. The Greeks, whether for aesthetic or for practical reasons, preferred to keep such scenes altogether out of sight. Modern audiences prefer to see rather more. The shadow device, as well as solving the problem of vocal identification, offered an acceptable compromise between the ancient idea and the modern. The shadows made the scene visually interesting as well as emotionally stirring, without running the risk of absurdity that might have occurred if the murder had been shown in full detail. In such scenes, what is suggested is always much more sinister than what is shown, and the shadow screen suggested precisely enough.

For me one of the chief attractions of the one-man performance has been the direct relationship that the performer can establish with his audience, and the liberty thus permitted him in modifying the details of his performance to respond to each audience's mood. Of course, the main lines of each production are worked out and set in rehearsal. There are features in the performance which must remain constant, and which cannot be changed without damage to the concept of the work as a whole. Yet within these limits there are many subtle modifications which can and should be made to conform with changing audience reactions. These changes may come about for various reasons. They may have to do with the age-group to which the audience belongs, or with its geographical location.

When I play *Medea* for high school audiences, I do not play it in the same way as I would before an adult group. For example, there is a long speech toward the end of the play, delivered by a messenger, describing the deaths of Jason's new bride and her father. Medea, feigning reconciliation, has sent the princess a robe and diadem impregnated with deadly poison; this is one part of the revenge that she plans against her husband. It is a horrible speech. Euripides describes graphically and with no detail spared, how the poison worked upon the princess, tearing her flesh from her bones, making her eyes start from their sockets, and so rending her that those around cannot bear to look at her. Although he loved the sensational, Euripides has not inserted this speech simply for cheap effect. It is a vital part of the play, and demonstrates the lengths to which Medea, in her hatred, is prepared to go to work vengeance on those she loved; she here sacrifices an innocent and unsuspecting girl to further a personal feud. But it is a speech which, from the nature of the description, walks the razor's edge between tragedy and absurdity. An adult audience, emotionally mature and theatrically sophisticated, will respond to it in the right way. A group of adolescents, less experienced and, usually, less acquainted with the nature of violence, will often be uneasy and respond with laughter —the laughter not of humor but of nervousness, born out of the desire to reject the, to them, unfair emotional demands that they feel the speech is making. So for this kind of audience I find it necessary to deliver the speech in a different way, hastening over potentially dangerous ground and deliberately underplaying what for an adult audience I would play for its full effect.

There are other dangers in performing to school audiences, which almost every performer will have experienced: not least, the possibility of touching innocently on some private joke, some local humor, that has nothing to do with the play at all. I recall sitting through a showing of the film *Hamlet*, with a mainly high school audience, in which the lines were rendered inaudible by the roar of laughter that went up with every iteration of the name "Gertrude." These accidents of production appear most frequently among young audiences, but are by no means confined to them. My point is that it is far easier for a solo performer to sense such a situation and adjust to it than for a whole cast to do so. In live production the rapport between performers is a very delicate thing, achieved at the cost of long rehearsal, and difficult to adjust on the spur of the moment. With one performer there is no such problem, and for this reason I would always advocate that the number involved in a marionette company be kept as small as possible, to facilitate communication both among themselves and between them and their audience.

Earlier in this chapter I mentioned the social and geographical factors involved in audience response to comedy. One audience will laugh where another will not. What causes hysteria in Halifax may fall flat in Milwaukee. What an audience of university professors finds amusing will bore a high school class. I have found that in performing classical comedy —particularly Aristophanes, whose comic structure is strange to moderns—that one can never predict a response, and that it is safe only to expect the unexpected. One never knows. The best audiences I have had for Aristophanes have been groups who had never seen his works, or even heard of the author, before they saw my version of *The Birds*, and so had no preconceptions. My most difficult audience was probably also the most eminent—an assembly of university teachers many of whom had been working on the plays for so long that Aristophanes for them had ceased to be a comedian and had become simply a compiler of textual problems. Any experienced actor can sense the attitude of his audience within a few minutes of stepping onto the stage, but it is very difficult for a whole company to modify the mood and tempo of their performance to suit. This is something that can be achieved by companies that have worked together for a long while and can react instinctively and corporately to any change of pace or emphasis; probably the Italian Commedia dell'Arte remains the supreme example of this approach to acting and production. In my own medium, I feel that I have been able to achieve this, and have found it, particularly in educational theatre, to be of real value.

I have tried to show throughout this chapter what the marionette may take from the live stage and what it may not. Puppetry, like cinema, is an art with strong affinities with the live theatre, but, also like cinema, it must learn to stand on its own feet and evolve its own techniques. Only then will the marionette stage develop its own serious dramatic literature, which will have as much, and as little, relationship to drama as we now know it as a shooting script by Ingmar Bergman has to a play by Shakespeare.

# The Plates

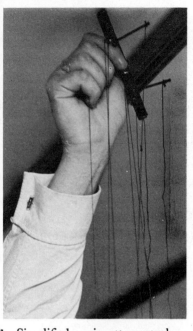

1  Simplified marionette control

2  The author with partially assembled marionette stage and figures from Euripides' *Medea*

3  Sophocles, *Oedipus the King:* Oedipus

4  Oedipus and his children

5  Creon            6  The Messenger from            7  Jocasta
                        Corinth

8  Racine, *Phèdre:* Phèdre and Hippolytus

9  Racine, *Phèdre:* Phèdre and Theseus

10  Sophocles, *Oedipus the King:*
Oedipus and Jocasta

11 Sophocles, *Oedipus the King:* the author, with final tableau. Note the use of different levels

12 Sophocles, *Oedipus the King:* the laying of the curse. Note the ramp leading up to stage level

13   Molière, *Les Fourberies de Scapin:* the opening scene, with Sylvester, Octavio, and Scapin

MOLIÈRE, *LES FOURBERIES DE SCAPIN*·

14 Leander, one of the young lovers

15 Argante, in the costume of the Italian Dottore, and Scapin

16 Geronte, in the traditional costume of Pantalone

17   Final tableau

18   Zerbinetta, the gypsy girl

19   Octavio, one of the young lovers

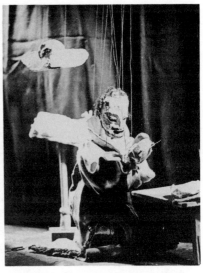

20  Molière, *Les Fourberies*
    *de Scapin:* Sylvester

21  Marlowe, *Doctor Faustus:* the
    Good Angel pleads with Faustus

22  Marlowe, *Doctor Faustus:* the meeting of the
    magicians. Cornelius, Valdes, and Faustus

**23** Faustus on the balcony    **24** The conjuration of Mephistopheles

MARLOWE, *DOCTOR FAUSTUS*

**25** The apparition of the Seven Deadly Sins

# 4

# The Play in Production

In this chapter I wish to trace the history of a complete production from the choice of play to the finished performance, and to discuss the various factors that influenced me at
each step of the way, the specific problems that arose, and the
solutions, more or less successful, that were found. This will,
I hope, serve both as an illustration of the general principles
outlined earlier in this book, and also as a practical guide for
those contemplating similar productions of their own. It is
neither possible nor desirable to lay down rules for production, in this or in any other type of theatre; the analysis given
here represents one man's approach to a particular play, and
if it serves only as a basis for criticism it will have achieved its
purpose.

In examining my repertoire for one production which
could most profitably be subjected to such analysis, and best
demonstrate the values and the difficulties of staging in this
medium, I have selected an Elizabethan tragedy, *The Tragical
History of Doctor Faustus*, by Christopher Marlowe. This
choice was dictated partly by affection. *Faustus* was my first
production of any play in this form, originally in a simplified
version; I later gave it the more elaborate revival which is

discussed here. More relevant to the present purpose, it demonstrates in several conspicuous ways, and perhaps more
clearly than works of other periods, how the peculiar qualities of the marionette may be used to solve urgent problems
of play revival, and to draw from the work associations that
it must have had at first appearance but which tend to be obscured in modern full-stage presentations.

SELECTION OF THE PLAY

Why did I first choose to present *Faustus*? Principally because it seemed to me that here was a striking instance of a
major work that had been neglected; the marionette stage
could repair the omission of its human counterpart. In its own
time the play was a great popular favorite. The confused state
of the text is itself a tribute to this popularity; it was several
times revised to suit the shifting tastes of new audiences, and
to introduce fresh topicalities. In Marlowe's time the author
held no copyright; the better received a play was, and the
longer it remained in the company's repertoire, the more
likely it was to suffer rewriting and interpolation. Today
*Doctor Faustus* is regularly read and studied as one of the
masterpieces of its own and of all time, but is only infre-
quently revived on the stage. This seemed to be sufficient
justification for performing the play, irrespective of the medium, in order that audiences might be permitted to see and
evaluate for themselves in performance a work they would
otherwise know only from the printed page. At the least, such
a production in marionette form would serve as a useful educational aid.

This was not the only reason. The story of Faustus has its
origins in early folklore, and has always been particularly
popular in Germany. It was from a German source that Marlowe took his own version; and in that country it has a traditional association with puppets. A popular version of the play

has been in the repertoire of German puppetmasters for centuries. In these traditional performances the comic element is often allowed to take precedence over the tragic, and Faustus' servant—often Kasperl, the German Punch—is elevated to the status of a major character. Marlowe's tragic version had its own influence on this folk-play, and it was by such a performance that Goethe was inspired to write his own massive *Faust*. It semed to me that this long relationship could not be accidental, and that there must be some innate sympathy between the material and my own medium which could be turned to good account in Marlowe's play.

The chief reason for this affinity should be immediately obvious: it lies in the magical nature of the play, and Marlowe relies no less on magic than do his German counterparts. In Marlowe's version we have, on the serious level, the various conjurations of the devils—Mephistopheles himself, and the spirits which Mephistopheles, Lucifer, and Beelzebub later produce—the apparitions of Helen of Troy and of Alexander the Great and his paramour, and the spectacle of the Seven Deadly Sins. On the semi-serious or comic level there are the devils that Wagner conjures up to scare the Clown, Robin and Ralph with their magic book, the banquet at which Pope and Cardinal are plagued by an invisible Faustus, the horse-courser and the incident of Faustus' detachable leg, and others.

In Marlowe's play this magic is not merely a decorative appendage, a show of conjuring tricks added for popular appeal, but an integral part of the play's thought. *Doctor Faustus* was written for an audience that believed in the possibilities of magic and alchemy, and accepted the existence of a personal Devil—not, perhaps, to the same extent as their medieval ancestors, but the belief was still there, and could be taken for granted by Marlowe when he composed his play. It is in this respect that the work presents critical problems in revival. The audience must accept a world in which such things exist before the play can have its full meaning. If we do not take Mephistopheles seriously, then we cannot take Faustus' contract seriously either, and he loses tragic stature. This is not to say that the play has nothing to say to those who do not believe in devils. The central theme of the man who overreaches himself and squanders those gifts that he has spent his soul to gain is still relevant and meaningful, but its effect is more powerful if Mephistopheles is as real to the audience as Faustus. *Macbeth* loses little by the exclusion of the witches; remove the diabolical element from *Faustus* and you lose a great deal. It is noticeable that several of the more important revivals of *Doctor Faustus* have recognized this discrepancy between Elizabethan and modern attitudes, and, while retaining the greater part of Marlowe's text, have tried to convey Faustus' lust for power, and his involvement in forces that ultimately destroy him, by other means. During the Second World War, Faustus was portrayed as a Nazi, twisting the text to show a man who is destroyed by political temptations; the learned Doctor of Wittenberg has more recently been depicted as an atomic scientist, a substitution of the new alchemy for the old.

Thus the difficulty is not simply the result of changing beliefs on the part of the audience. One of the functions, and the powers, of theatre is to make credible to an audience a world they do not normally inhabit. But the attitude to the stage, and particularly to stage spectacle, has also changed. The Elizabethan audiences were sympathetic to the limitations of stage illusion. Stage magic could be presented to them by a few fairly simple mechanical devices, and they would lend it their credence. They would not ask for complete realism; given the hint, their imaginations would do the rest. This is not to suggest that Marlowe's audiences were naïve; they certainly were not. But they did have a different attitude to what they saw on the stage, and to what they could expect from it. It was possible for Marlowe, without straining the resources of his theatre unduly, to create a diabolical world that was completely convincing. This is no longer so easy.

Modern audiences, conditioned by the total realism of film and television, tend to be less imaginative and less tolerant; they also tend to be more knowledgeable about the ways in which effects are produced. Accustomed to Superman, they will be more critical of Wagner's Valkyries suspended on wires which are not only visible but prone to mechanical failure. After viewing the monsters of the past, present, and future worlds which science fiction, abetted by the camera, can conjure up for us, they will be less moved by the stage serpent with which Tamino struggles at the opening of *The Magic Flute*. (One might ask, parenthetically; if this effect is ever, or can ever be, convincingly produced on the modern stage? I have seen it done in many ways—a huge canvas shape with men inside; reduced to the size of a smallish python, so that Tamino could wrestle with it and give it some semblance of life with his own hands; draped on the boughs of a tree, and motionless, so that Tamino's emotion, and gratitude at his rescue, seemed rather excessive; and even wholly imaginary, with the Three Ladies reduced to making wild thrusts with their spears at no apparent object. The only convincing serpent I have yet seen was in Herr Aicher's marionette production at Salzburg. Here Tamino and the serpent inhabited the same world, and competed on equal terms.) A live production must always fight against this difficulty. If the effects are badly contrived they will not carry conviction, and if well, the audience is likely to spend so much time wondering how they are done that the play will be forgotten.

As I earlier suggested in the first chapter, the puppet, by his nature, removes this difficulty. He is by definition a being apart. His world is not our world, and he is capable of many things beyond the scope of human beings. He can levitate himself and fly, he can shrink and expand, he can collapse and reassemble himself. Thus an audience, watching such things in puppet performance, will not be too much concerned with technical achievements or the lack of them. In the first place the effects can be contrived more easily, and in the second they are innate to the medium, part of the puppet's law of being, so that the magic will not attract disproportionate interest. The "willing suspension of disbelief" is facilitated, the magic is taken for granted, and the rest of the performance may proceed unimpaired.

Besides the magical quality of *Faustus*, and hardly less important, is the aspect of characterization. In writing his play Marlowe was under a heavy debt to the Middle Ages, both in his stage effects and in his conception of his characters. Apart from Faustus himself, and to a lesser extent the devil who tempts him, few of the characters are conceived as fully-rounded human beings. This is as true of Marlowe's tragedy as it is of the traditional folk-play. Marlowe created a Doctor Faustus who is three-dimensional, who has a heart and a soul, who is for the audience a vivid personality. He thinks, he reasons, he is tormented by conflicting desires; he has a choice to make—or rather, as Marlowe sees it, a series of choices—and in each case he chooses wrongly. Mephistopheles, the diabolical servant who becomes his master, also reveals something of this complexity. Under the conventional satanic mask lies a pathos, even a tragedy, of the fallen angel. Mephistopheles' lament for Paradise lost at the beginning of the play is hardly less moving than Faustus' at its end. Modern actors have tended to exploit this aspect of the character, notably Robert Eddison, who has made Mephistopheles a figure out of Milton rather than out of Marlowe, a tragic character so dominant that he divides the honors with Faustus himself.

But this complexity is nowhere to be found in the rest of the large cast. Faustus is a Renaissance man, with his expansiveness of spirit, his zest for power and experience, and his

faith in the ultimate triumph of human knowledge and reason. The minor characters come from the Middle Ages, or
more specifically from the medieval morality play, in which
the characters are not people but abstractions, personifications
of types of virtue and vice. They fall into two main groups, the
wholly good and the wholly evil. This may be seen most
clearly in the Good and Evil Spirits, whom Marlowe uses to
externalize and make visible the conflict in Faustus' mind.
Valdes and Cornelius, the two sorcerers, are evil forces, and
the Old Man who counsels Faustus to repentance is a power
for good. This rudimentary black-and-white characterization,
though it presents problems for the modern actor, is of the
essence of puppetry. The puppet can symbolize and caricature. It is perhaps significant that when Orson Welles produced his version of *Doctor Faustus* he had several characters
portrayed by life-size puppets, and this was felt by critics to
be completely in harmony with the play's style. We are presented with the picture of an individual torn between conflicting forces, and the importance of Faustus' dilemma is
seen most clearly when these forces are presented as imper-
sonally as possible. Once again, the puppet can prove its value.
As in the Greek plays, it is desirable that the human element
should not unduly intrude, and it is this quality of abstraction
that the puppet, by its nature, can so well provide.

### PREPARATION OF THE TEXT

*Doctor Faustus* has come down to us in two principal versions, the quarto of 1604—the earliest printed text that we
have, reprinted in 1609 and 1611—and the greatly expanded
version of 1616. There has been considerable scholarly argument over how much of these texts is by Marlowe, and how
much represents additions and interpolations by later hands.
Two main points emerge. Firstly, in neither version do we
have an accurate transcription of what was performed in Mar-

lowe's lifetime. Secondly, the earlier and shorter version is likely to be closer to the play as it was first written. It is this version, on which most modern editors have based their texts, that I have used as the core of the marionette production. For the purposes of the following account, it will be assumed that readers are familiar with the play, or have a text at hand. Scene-divisions are numbered according to the Folger Library General Reader's edition.*

The play falls naturally into three parts. The first shows Faustus' decision to practice the black arts and his signing of a pact with the Devil. Next comes a group of scenes in which Faustus is revealed in the full enjoyment of his magic powers. Finally we are shown the expiration of the bond, Faustus' tardy repentance, and his descent into Hell. Throughout the play, comic scenes, several involving Faustus' servant Wagner, are interwoven with the tragic. These serve both as light relief and as a sardonic comment on the tragic scenes; often the comedy makes the same point as the tragic scene that has preceded it, though in a different mood.

The cutting of the text was dictated largely by practical necessity. A one-man performance imposes certain limitations of endurance, and in practice it has been found that a performance length of approximately one and a half hours is ideal. It was also necessary to reduce the cast to such proportions that the production could travel easily, and for the same reason to eliminate any scenes or parts of scenes which would necessitate bulky scenery or properties. I attempted, therefore, while observing these limitations, to prepare a version which would still preserve the full flavor of Marlowe's play, both in its comic and its tragic aspects, and, in particular, retain the full tragic sweep of Faustus' rise and fall. This resulted in the following text:

* Christopher Marlowe, *The Tragedy of Doctor Faustus*, ed. Louis B. Wright and Virginia Lamar, Folger Library General Reader's Edition (New York: Washington Square Press, 1959).

*Prologue*

*Scene 1*: Faustus in his study; his review of his career, his decision to take up black magic and his meeting with Valdes and Cornelius.

*Scene 2*: Wagner's mockery of the Scholars.

*Scene 3*: Faustus' conjuration of Mephistopheles.

*Scene 4*: Wagner binds the Clown to his service.

*Scene 5*: Faustus in his study; the signing of the bond.

*Scene 6*: Faustus' half-repentance, the appearance of Lucifer and Beelzebub, and the pageant of the Seven Deadly Sins.

*Scene 7*: The Papal Banquet.

*Scene 12*: Faustus' magical presentation of grapes to the Duchess of Vanholt.

*Scene 13*: The confrontation between Faustus and the Old Man, who urges repentance; the apparition of Helen of Troy.

*Scene 14*: Faustus' appeal to the Scholars, his last hour on earth, and his descent to Hell.

*Epilogue*

After the first few performances, the play was shortened even further by the omission of the Papal Banquet and the Vanholt scenes, the latter because of the pressure of time and the former from dissatisfation with the staging of so elaborate a scene in this medium. When *Faustus* was written the audience, still strongly conscious of its new Protestantism and tending to equate the Papacy with England's enemies, would have rejoiced at the scene in which the learned Doctor makes himself invisible and robs the Pope of his food, and even more at the sequence which follows, in which a group of corpulent monks are scared out of their wits by devils and fireworks. In our more tolerant age the scene has lost its topicality and much of its spice. It can still succeed in a live production, but only when its dated content can be disguised with spectacular staging and comic business. Such things are beyond the scope of the miniature theatre, and it was thought best to eliminate the scene altogether. This left a version which covered only the first and third sections of Marlowe's play, but which was still self-contained, which still preserved a measure of spectacle in the Seven Deadly Sins sequence, and which was leavened with broad humor. This text has a playing time of one hour and ten minutes, and has proved extremely successful in performance.

THE SETTING

The largest audiences for my performances are drawn from university groups who are interested in the plays as historical material as well as for their inherent dramatic interest. I normally attempt, therefore, to utilize a setting which is at least based on the original. In *Doctor Faustus* an approximation of the "typical" Elizabethan stage was used. It makes no claim to be historically accurate, but rather to show how a permanent architectural setting, involving a number of fixed elements, can be used to provide all the locations that so complex a play requires.

The setting involves a two-storied façade, painted in false perspective. Various views of this may be seen in the accompanying illustrations (plates 21-25). It is constructed in three sections for easy transportation. The two side panels, on which the doors are painted, are bolted to the stage floor, and the balcony is connected across them by a simple slot-and-tongue arrangement; when removed, the balcony can be folded into about one-third of its open length. This simple setting offers a choice of three acting areas, the inner stage, the main stage, and the balcony. The balcony, of course, is left floorless, to allow figures to be manipulated within the inner stage. Properties are similarly simple. The inner stage is set permanently as Faustus' study, with a bench and a lectern. One end of the bench is left clear for Faustus to sit on, and a book lies open at the other; this is fastened down, as all small properties should be on the marionette stage, for safety's sake. Another book lies open on the lectern (see plate 21). The trap, part of the permanent stage fittings (see plate 25) is used for hellish appearances and disappearances, as described below.

### THE LIGHTING

The main stage and inner stage are lit separately. One flood, with yellow filter to suggest candlelight, illuminates the inner stage, the "study." Three white floods and one blue light the main stage; the blue is used together with the white for extra illumination in "daylight" scenes, and independently for "night" scenes and magic effects. The balcony has no special lighting; little of the action takes place here, and enough light spills from the main areas to cover it. Two special effects lanterns supply red light for the Hell scenes. One is located on floor level down stage right (i.e., serving as a single footlight) and the other beneath the trap. Specific areas were lighted only at the beginning of scenes, to indicate where the action was supposed to be taking place. Once this had been established, the general illumination was brought up. For instance, at the beginning of Scene 1 Faustus is revealed sitting in his study, lit only by the one yellow flood; after a few lines of his soliloquy the main stage lighting comes up, so that the whole stage is illuminated. With the exit of Valdes and Cornelius the main stage darkens again until only the study is visible for Faustus' last lines.

### THE CHARACTERS

In selecting prototypes for the marionettes, several sources suggested themselves. The 1624 edition of the play has a woodcut of Faustus (probably intended to represent Edward Alleyn, who created the part) conjuring up the devil. The figure of Faustus himself was copied from this. Other figures, like Valdes, Cornelius, and the Scholars, were taken from the conventionalized representations on Elizabethan and Jacobean tombs, which seemed to have just the degree of formality that I was seeking. In creating the Good and Evil Angels and the Seven Deadly Sins Marlowe drew heavily on medieval sources; it was therefore thought appropriate to find inspiration for these figures in the conventions of medieval illustration. They will be discussed in more detail in the scene-analysis below.

## THE PRODUCTION

*Prologue*: Spoken by an anonymous Chorus, this is not part of the play proper, but a formal introduction of the play to the audience, an appeal for a favorable hearing, and a relation of a certain amount of essential background information. In the context of the marionette production, it seemed appropriate to have the operator, as actor, speak this prologue directly to the audience without the intermediary of the puppet stage. This not only stresses the formality of the prologue device but provides the audience with a bridge between the live theatre, with which they are more familiar, and the puppets themselves. They move from consideration of the living actor to the marionette, and thus enter more easily into a form in which they are probably not used to seeing serious plays presented. The prologue can also be blocked in such a way as to help the audience adjust its focus from the larger stage to the small area on which it will be concentrating for the next hour.

The staging of the prologue necessarily varies from place to place and from hall to hall, but ideally I like to stage it as follows, using the lighting resources of the full stage as well as my own. I begin the prologue in full view of the audience and and as far downstage as possible, gradually moving backward toward the puppet stage as the speech proceeds. Simultaneously, the stage lighting dims until, on the line "But surfeits upon cursed necromancy," there is complete darkness, and I am in position ready to operate. With the last line of the prologue, "And this the man that in his study sits," the lighting comes up in the study to reveal Faustus already seated, and the play proper begins. This interaction between the human and the marionette can be very exciting, and is used again, for a different purpose, later in the play.

I have found such focus-adjusting devices useful, and employ them wherever I can, though their precise nature changes from play to play. It is hard to expect the audience to adjust immediately, as soon as the house lights are dimmed, from the large hall to the tiny rectangle where the action is, and anything which can make this transition easier is worth investigating. In Aristophanes' *The Birds* I begin the play in complete darkness; the lights do not come up on the marionette stage until six or eight lines have been spoken. This gives the audience an opportunity to adjust themselves mentally before they have to adjust their eyes.

*Scene 1*: Only the study is lit at first; this establishes location, as previously described.

*Settle thy studies, Faustus* . . . Faustus is seated on the bench.

*Sweet Analytics, 'tis thou hast ravished me!* Still seated, Faustus turns and looks down, to read the book on the bench by his side.

*Galen come* . . . He rises, moves across to the lectern, and reads the book there.

*Is not thy common talk sound aphorisms?* Faustus, full of his own glory, turns away from the lectern and speaks straight at the audience. Lights up on main stage.

*Physic, farewell. Where is Justinian?* Turns back to lectern, reads.

*Jerome's Bible, Faustus, view it well.* Back to bench, kneels to read book there (see plate 21).

*These metaphysics of magicians . . .* Speaks the rest of the
   speech gazing offstage left.
*Here, Faustus, try thy brains to gain a deity!* Back to bench,
   sits.

In this sequence a long speech is broken up by using as much
movement as possible within the confines of the study. Faustus is continually turning from one side to another, and moving from place to place; this helps to convey his restlessness
and spiritual dissatisfaction. Note also that this scene offers an
excellent illustration of the way in which setting and properties must be simplified for marionette purposes. The action
calls for Faustus to be seen in his study surrounded by the
apparatus of scholarship; he considers one branch of learning
after another, finally to reject all for black magic. In a live production the designer will make full use of his opportunities,
introducing books, globes, and charts, sometimes even retorts
and skeletons, and the director will devise appropriate business to make use of these. But what is meaningful and interesting on the live stage would be a pointless clutter here. In my
production Faustus has simply two books, one open on the
bench, one on the lectern. This makes the necessary point
without overelaboration; we have to see Faustus first reading,
and then turning away from his books. No member of the
audience has ever objected that the same book is used to represent the works of Aristotle and Jerome's Bible, or for both
Galen and Justinian. Either they do not notice—which I suspect to be the truth—or they accept it as a necessary convention.

*Wagner, commend me to my dearest friends . . .* Wagner has
   been in position just offstage from the beginning of the
   play, ready for a quick entrance. He enters stage right when
   called, takes up his position behind the lectern, bows, re-
   ceives his instructions and withdraws. Although he has only
   three words to say—"I will, sir,"—it is as well to use some

trick of voice or gesture to make them funny, thus preparing the audience for the use of Wagner as a comic character later on.

*Enter the* Good Angel *and the* Evil Angel. As I have noted above, this is a device that Marlowe borrows from the religious drama of the Middle Ages. The Angels reappear throughout the play at moments when Faustus' spiritual crisis is most intense. They represent the two conflicting strains in his character. First one, then the other whispers to him; the Evil Angel always offers material temptation, and it is to him that Faustus ultimately listens. In live productions these appearances are difficult to stage. They must be very rapid, and there is the further problem of the "magic" element that I have already discussed. But this is puppetry, and live-stage limitations do not apply. As the Angels are a medieval device, it seemed both useful and appropriate to adopt a visual solution drawn from medieval painting. The Angels are represented not as complete figures, as they would have to be in a live production, but as winged heads in appropriate colors—Good white and gold, Evil red and purple. Nor do they enter in the conventional manner; they descend, to hover around Faustus' head like the familiar angels and cherubs of religious art (see plate 21). By this means all their entrances and exits can be made almost instantaneous, as well as being in perfect visual accord with the mood of the scene. I had earlier used the same method to represent the various spiritual attributes in the medieval *Everyman*, where it proved equally successful.

*How am I glutted with conceit of this!* As the Evil Angel ascends, Faustus rises, and delivers his next speech directly at the audience.

*Enter Valdes and Cornelius.* They enter together main stage right, and bow. Faustus crosses the study to their side. Although they are separated by the barrier of the scenic façade, Valdes and Cornelius play the whole scene as close to the study as possible, thus giving, with Faustus, the effect of a tight group.

*Know that your words have won me at the last*

*To practice magic and concealed arts.* Valdes and Cornelius turn to look at each other.

*Faustus, these books, thy wit* . . . Valdes crosses left to the far side of the stage and turns; Faustus is thus framed between Valdes and Cornelius as they tempt him, and turns from one to the other to hear them speak.

*Then haste thee to some solitary grove* . . . Both Valdes and Cornelius move closer to Faustus; their voices drop to a whisper.

*Then come and dine with me* . . . Valdes crosses back right to Cornelius; they bow and retire while Faustus is still speaking. This avoids the mechanical problem of having three marionettes leave the stage at the same time, and throws all the emphasis on Faustus for the crucial last line of the scene. As he speaks, the lights darken on the main stage; as he makes his exit the study too darkens.

The remaining scenes will not be analyzed in the same detail; only the most noteworthy features of each scene will be listed.

*Scene 2*: Lights come up again on the main stage, where the meeting between Wagner and the Scholars is played. The Scholars enter left, Wagner right. After their confrontation, Wagner leaves in the direction from which he came. The Scholars, talking sadly of Faustus' fall from grace, cross the stage slowly from left to right and so exeunt. As they do so, the white floods go out, leaving only the blue in readiness for the conjuration scene that follows.

*Scene 3*: Faustus enters main stage right, and plays in this general position throughout. Mephistopheles appears main stage left—in medieval practice, the traditional "evil" side. He appears in two incarnations, and so two figures must be made for him. His first manifestation, in his full hellish shape, is modelled after the figure of the devil in the 1624 woodcut described earlier. For this entrance he descends from above, to be seen only momentarily as he hangs poised in midair. Here flashes of lightning provide the chief illumination; in this production the magic scenes were regularly underlit, on the principle that what the audience imagines is more terrible than what it sees. For his second entrance, as a Franciscan friar, Mephistopheles walks on in the normal way (see plate 24). At the conclusion of the dialogue Faustus exits stage right, and the lights come up full on the main stage.

*Scene 4*: Enter Clown stage left, Wagner stage right. This scene is a comic version of the conjuration we have already witnessed. It is therefore blocked in exactly the same way, with Wagner in Faustus' former position throughout. The devils, this time comic figures, drop to the stage from above. At the end of the scene, a brief blackout; then light again in the study.

*Scene 5*: The study alone is lit during Faustus' opening soliloquy and his first speeches to Mephistopheles. After the latter leaves to bring fire, he reappears on the main stage which is then lit blue. The various magic apparitions—the "devil dressed as a woman with fireworks" and the "show of spirits" (in this production a box of treasure and rich fabrics which slowly descends and opens) both appear on the main stage. One important point arises from this scene. According to the text, a number of small hand properties are required— the knife with which Faustus cuts his arm, the fire that Mephistopheles brings to warm his blood, the bond that Faustus signs, the magic book that he is given. Such things could be contrived mechanically, but would take more trouble than they are worth. In practice it was found perfectly satisfactory to leave them to the imagination of the audience. An evocative gesture, combined with the author's words, is quite sufficient, and no further illusion is required. A short blackout at the end of this scene indicates a lapse of time.

*Scene 6*: Faustus' speech of contrition and repentance is played on the main stage. Once again the Good and Evil Angels descend and circle around his head. When Faustus prays, the coming of Lucifer and Beelzebub is signaled by darkening the whole stage and bringing up the red flood downstage right. These characters presented a considerable problem. They are the only major diabolical figures who appear for any length of time in their proper shapes, and it is important that they be distinguished from the other characters in some significant way. In the first performances I used flat shapes designed to be seen in silhouette, hoping that this would impart the appropriate eeriness to their presence. This, however, was not entirely satisfactory, and I eventually resorted to a method which was first suggested by pure accident. The low-level lighting used for this scene could be arranged in such a way that I, standing over the stage, was partly illuminated. This, contrasted with the small scale of the marionettes, gave the suggestion of a monstrous presence brooding over the stage and the play. The device of contrasting human with puppet performers is one that most operators have used at one time or another, but mostly for comic effect. Many puppet troupes bring the manipulators onto the stage with their figures as a finale to the show, and the sudden readjustment from one scale to another rarely fails to raise a gasp from the audience. In this particular case the time-worn trick could be turned to genuine dramatic effect. I have since used it in other plays, particularly in Greek tragedy, where the sense of an indefinable presence brooding over the action can utilize the actual relationship between puppet and operator to convey the feeling, appropriate in this drama-form, that the characters are themselves subject to vaster powers, and caught up in an action over which they have no control.

The same scene contains the pageant of the Seven Deadly Sins, summoned from Hell for Faustus' entertainment. They emerged, appropriately, from the Hell-trap. Like the Good and Evil Angels, they were not complete figures but heads only; all seven were mounted in the correct order on two long strings, and loaded into the trap before the performance. By slowly pulling the strings the heads emerge one by one as their lines are spoken, lit partly by the red light from below the trap and partly by one of the main stage floods (see plate 25). The inspiration for modelling these heads came from yet another source, the paintings of Hieronymus Bosch, which provide a fruitful compendium of horrors. This is another instance of how a simple mechanical device can, in this medium, give complete conviction to a scene often difficult to handle in live-stage practice. The scene concludes with a brief blackout.

*Scene* 7: The main stage lights come up again. Wagner speaks his brief forecast of his master's death from the balcony. Faustus and the students enter main stage left; when he accedes to their request to show them Helen of Troy, all lights fade except blue. Like the other apparitions in the play, Helen is not a complete figure; she does not even have a face. Every man has his own image of Helen of Troy, his own standard of perfect beauty, and whether you make Helen a blonde or a brunette you risk alienating half your audience. My Helen had no face, merely the suggestion of a face; nor did she have a body, merely a swirl of translucent draperies. The suggestion is enough, and the audience can supply the rest for themselves. Once again the marionette shows its value in abstracting, in suggesting rather than stating. Incidentally, the same reasoning applied to the construction of Mephistopheles as friar. It is impossible to represent satisfactorily on the stage either consummate beauty or consummate evil. Mephistopheles, like Helen, had no face within his friar's cowl, only a dark void.

*Scene 8*: The final scene of the play, in which Faustus

passes the last hour of his earthly life, utilizes the full resources of the stage. Faustus' long soliloquy begins on the main stage; as it proceeds, he passes behind the painted door to ascend into the balcony. It is here that he makes his invocation to the stars. This over, he descends again, and gradually works his way across the stage until he is standing by the trap. In the original production I had included all the taped sound effects that I could muster—the clock striking first eleven, then the half-hour, then twelve, wind, thunder, and a culminating diabolical scream. Partly in the course of rehearsals, and partly in the first few performances, I came to realize that, once again, I could make a greater impression by understatement. We do not know how many sound effects were used in the original production; I ended by using none, and in fact none are needed. Marlowe's words are enough to convey the pity and terror of Faustus' situation. I eventually eliminated even the striking clock as distracting, signifying the passage of time by a sharp dimming of the lights on the half-hour; the rest of the soliloquy was spoken in the blue light only, and this too was extinguished at the end of the speech, so that Faustus was illuminated solely by the red glow spreading from the slowly opening trap. As Faustus makes his last despairing appeal, he falls into the trap, which closes upon him. For this it was necessary to drop the puppet, control and all. This is something which, according to the manuals, one should never do, but in this case the end justified the means. In fact, there have been very few occasions on which the strings have been hopelessly tangled afterwards.

*Epilogue*: This is spoken in complete darkness.

In the last analysis, it is impossible to convey the effect of a stage production on paper. However, I hope that the foregoing description will have suggested a possible approach toward presenting a play of this type, and solutions to the problems presented by this and other works. My own experience with the play was a happy and productive one, and helped me to formulate some of the ideas which I now feel to be fundamental to the art of puppetry. The puppeteer often finds himself in the position of the cinema in its earliest years, namely, of being in thrall to the live theatre. The first temptation is always to copy live theatre practice, to construct a miniature stage and a replica of a live-stage set, and to offer what is simply a scaled-down version of a live production. In time, one realizes that this will not do; there are other possibilities and other solutions. The marionette theatre can draw heavily on techniques from the non-theatrical arts, particularly from painting, which are impossible on the live stage. The puppeteer must learn to create his own conventions, and not follow slavishly those already laid down by other media. The aim must be to simplify as much as possible, and to eliminate any effect which is not absolutely essential to the production. This type of production could be described as reader's theatre with visual aids; yet I feel that its approach is more likely to be historically correct than one employing all the scenic resources of the full theatre, and that it places the spectator in a position more closely approximating that in which he would have found himself in Marlowe's own time.

# 5

## Some Applications and Conclusions

In the foregoing chapters I have endeavored to demonstrate some of the aesthetic advantages that the marionette stage can offer, and the values that it can contribute to the performance of serious drama. There are certain other advantages, particularly in the realm of education, that deserve notice.

The first and most obvious of these is the advantage of portability. In these days of rising stage costs, any method that assists audiences remote from the chief theatrical centers to become acquainted with the masterpieces of world drama is worth considering. Even those who look on the puppet theatre as an inferior alternative to live performance must admit that it is possible to bring works in this medium to audiences who would otherwise never see them. I have always considered as one of the most practical advantages of my work the ease with which I could bring such plays as *Oedipus the King*, *Doctor Faustus*, and *Phèdre* to groups to whom they would normally be completely inaccessible, and who in some cases would never see live theatre at all. With marionettes this can be done at a fraction of the cost of importing a live company, even where such a company can be found. The marionette theatre asks little in the way of facilities or accommodation. It can be erected in a full-size theatre or a classroom, a science lecture room or a village hall. In the course of the last seventeen years I have performed in almost every conceivable situation, from my own theatre at the Ashland Shakespeare Festival to the courtyard of an English farmhouse. Often the audience response has been most enthusiastic where the surroundings have been most primitive. Anyone who has taught courses in theatre history or dramatic literature knows that one performance, one visual demonstration, is worth twenty lectures, and for me there has been no experience quite so rewarding as that of bringing to life, for an audience of students, a play that they have hitherto known only as words on a printed page. Even in those places that have ample access to live theatre, many of the works commonly studied as set texts can never now be seen in performance. The English-speaking theatre, for instance, is notoriously shy of Racine and Corneille, and even the Greeks, apart from a handful of plays, have been conspicuously neglected. The marionette theatre, at the very least, offers a way of filling this gap which can be exploited by individual performers, by companies, or by whole classes working together on a common project.

Then there is the opportunity of staging plays which, although retaining considerable literary and historical appeal, are never performed, even in university theatres, because they lack the popular interest which would justify the expense of a major revival. I mentioned in Chapter One the Lanchesters' production of *L'Amfiparnaso,* which brought to a wide public a work which would otherwise have continued to languish in obscurity. The Salzburg Marionette Theatre has performed a similar service for some of Mozart's minor operas, exquisite pieces but rarely, because of their unfamiliarity, attempted by live companies. This field is a wide one, and should recommend itself to teachers of the drama. The range of Elizabethan theatre alone suggests many examples. It is almost impossible nowadays to go through life without seeing a performance of Shakespeare, in some medium or other. Even Marlowe and Webster are occasionally given their due. But who performs Heywood, Kyd, Greene, or Tourneur? Where can a student hope to see *The Spanish Tragedy*, *Gorboduc*, or *James IV*? How often, in the English-speaking theatre, can one find productions of Terence, Lope de Vega, Marivaux, or Alfieri? The works of all these dramatists could, with suitable adaptation—in some cases, with very little—find a place in the marionette repertoire. There is also a case for presenting in this way the unfamiliar works of major dramatists. It is usually possible to see *Le Bourgeois Gentilhomme* or *Tartuffe*, but *Psyche*, the tragedy-ballet which Molière wrote in collaboration with Corneille, and which in so many ways sums up the spirit of his age, has vanished from the theatre. Its limited appeal and elaborate mythological spectacle have denied it live revival, but it would fit easily into the compass of the marionette theatre. It would be good to see the puppets used as an adjunct to a live university theatre program, and devoted to works of more specialized scholarly or historical interest.

One might also include here those works whose dramatic interest has been outweighed by the impossibility of providing the elaborate production they demand. Many plays of considerable merit go without production for generations, even for centuries, because their authors have allowed their flow of imagination to carry them beyond what is practical. The works of Seneca might be considered here, and Byron, both of whom demand stage effects beyond the reach of most theatres. There are plays like Ibsen's *Caesar and Galilean*, a study of pagan and Christian mentalities in conflict—or even the same author's *Peer Gynt*, produced far less often than it deserves simply because of the difficulties of staging. But on the small scale of the puppet theatre all is possible. The puppeteer reckons in cents what would cost the live producer thousands of dollars, and he can change settings as easily as he can move the puppets themselves. It would be rewarding to see the great poetic dramas, like Goethe's *Faust*, of which Part One is seldom enough performed and Part Two hardly ever except as a dramatic reading, or Thomas Hardy's *The Dynasts*, in which the puppet could perform a tremendous service by making the rapid changes of scene, the jumps from fact to fancy, visually possible. The puppet stage has, in fact, many of the advantages of film and television combined; it can encompass a wide range of settings with the minimum delay, and can still keep the intimate personal rapport between performer and audience which is characteristic of live theatre.

X Apart from their value in making plays more accessible, I have found marionettes useful in breaking down the barrier that exists between modern audiences, particularly student audiences, and certain sorts of plays to which they have been insufficiently exposed. Modern audiences tend to be so conditioned by the realism to which they are accustomed on the film and television screen that they look suspiciously on any play that departs from the patterns with which they have become familiar. They are initially antagonistic to any play that employs formal devices, be it in writing, acting, or staging. It has often been noted that audiences will accept much more in the way of experiment and unorthodoxy from forms that are not considered "legitimate" theatre, such as the ballet and the musical, than they will from the straight play. In the musical, frankly presentational methods of stage setting are not only popularly acceptable but welcome. In *Guys and Dolls* a brief scene indicating a flight from New York to Havana was staged with perfect simplicity by flashing a "Fasten Your Seat Belts" sign on to the traverse curtain. In *Gypsy*, a car journey across the United States was staged with the principals in a stationary car and a number of extras walking across the stage bearing names of the towns supposed to be passed en route. In the non-musical play such devices are still considered somewhat revolutionary.

The same attitude is observable in the relationship of the audience to the puppet play. Theatrically unsophisticated spectators will accept much on the puppet stage that they would regard with suspicion if played by live actors. They accept from the beginning that puppets are unreal, and may therefore reasonably be expected to behave in an unrealistic way. I have already touched on this point in connection with the magic which is so important to *Doctor Faustus;* it is true in other ways also. The acceptance of the convention that live performers may be replaced by lay figures induces a readiness to accept other conventions of plot, staging, and characterization, though these are already inherent in the play and have nothing to do with the puppets. Once again, the "willing suspension of disbelief" is facilitated by the admitted artificiality of the medium. I have performed Greek tragedy and comedy to many unlikely audiences, particularly young audiences, who have come to my *Medea* because of the attraction of marionettes, where they would have avoided Judith Anderson in the same play for fear of seeing something "educational" which would bore them. And, once inside, they have begun by enjoying the marionettes and ended, often to their surprise, by enjoying Greek tragedy; the transition has been painless. In this way the puppeteer can trade on the traditional charm of his medium to introduce audiences to new theatrical experiences. The natural attractiveness of the puppet, the knowledge that anything is likely to happen, frees the mind of prejudice and preconceptions. Reluctance to come to terms with the unfamiliar has always been the live theatre's greatest enemy. With puppets this difficulty is smoothed over, mental barriers are broken down, and the instinctive hostility to unusual methods of staging or unfamiliar drama-forms does not occur.

I have found equally interesting results, and for the same

reasons, in presenting Racine. French neoclassical tragedy is perhaps the most conspicuous example of a type of drama whose attitudes, forms, and conventions are acceptable only with difficulty to readers and audiences of other countries. The traditional hostility of French critics to Shakespeare has been paralleled by the almost total indifference of English and American audiences to Racine and Corneille. These authors deal in a world that we must make a conscious effort of will to enter. This effort is for most of us difficult, and for many unrewarding. These are plays which conspicuously avoid physical action, even where such action seems to be demanded from the characters by the plot. Their characters conduct themselves according to a code of heroic behavior which, though valid for its own time and circle, seems to have little in common with the world as we know it. They speak a language which is deliberately artificial and—particularly in English translation—appears inflated and redundant. For this reason performances of such plays outside France are rare. It is occasionally possible to see a touring French actress in *Phèdre*, and university theatres sometimes stage other of Racine's plays, but these are performances for aficionados only, and cannot be said to command any widespread popular support. In the marionette theatre these problems are, as in the case of Greek tragedy, minimized. The formal language which falls unconvincingly from a live actor comes more acceptably from a character who is himself artificial. Action which is static and implausible on the full stage adapts more easily to its miniature counterpart. I suspect that it is in this field, that of formal, heroic tragedy, that the puppet theatre can make its greatest contribution. Several artists are currently working on such ideas; and this is something to which the marionette can contribute its own tradition of heroic drama, familiar in the old Sicilian and Italian performances.

I have tried to convey the idea of puppetry as a filter, a way of making more palatable drama-forms whose interest has declined on the live stage due to the disappearance of an acting tradition, or a revolution in modes of writing. Other examples come to mind. One of these is directly opposed to the style of Racine—the play of horror and violence found so frequently in the work of Elizabethan and Jacobean writers. Shakespeare's *Titus Andronicus,* his most popular play in his own time, usually fails dismally in revival because its action is no longer acceptable. We have here a play in which one horrible incident follows another. Titus loses his son and cuts off his own hand in full view of the audience. Lavinia is ravished and loses her tongue and hands. There is murder and infanticide, and the play ends with a Thyestean banquet in which no terror is spared. Modern audiences are less sympathetic to these cumulative horrors than their Elizabethan predecessors. Our own age, less familiar with daily violence, rejects the portrayal of so much violence on the stage, and finds merely ridiculous what the Elizabethans found moving. *Titus* has, in fact, become one of the classic failures of stage history. The only production in recent times to have achieved real success was the famous Laurence Olivier-Vivien Leigh-Peter Brook revival of 1957. This was almost entirely owing to the efforts of the director, who from the moment the curtain rose strove to establish a world—owing more, perhaps, to science fiction than to Shakespeare—which was neither Roman nor Elizabethan, but a nightmare land in which such events could be plausible. It is likely that, on the puppet stage, the artist could create this sense of a private, violent, and utterly plausible world just as effectively and more easily. The same could be done for a number of other works—Kyd's *The Spanish Tragedy* comes at once to mind—and so a whole new area of theatre could be opened up to audiences whose preconceptions have previously denied them this experience.

What is true of violence is also true of obscenity. I have found many times that the coarser jokes of, say, Aristophanes or Ben Jonson, often cut from live productions because of the embarrassment of the actors in speaking or of the audience in hearing them, can be retained in a puppet version of the same play without giving offence. In a word, what is unacceptable to modern audiences, for one reason or another, as part of live stage behavior can be rendered acceptable by utilizing a medium which is itself at one remove from reality.

The traditional puppet book concerns itself almost entirely with construction methods and operating techniques, and relegates material and presentation to a brief appendix. In reversing this procedure, I am conscious that I may have been equally unfair in the other direction. I remain convinced, however, that the question of suitable material is of vital importance if puppetry is ever to be taken seriously in the English-speaking world as a medium of dramatic expression. I have tried to show what has been accomplished, and what may be accomplished; to suggest that the puppet is no mere substitute for the live actor, any more than the film is a substitute for the live stage. Puppetry is no momentary diversion but a means of expression offering some things that the live theatre cannot give, in some ways its handmaid, in others its superior. The theories of such men as Craig cannot be lightly disregarded, nor can the critical eulogies lavished upon serious puppet productions. Whenever the puppet theatre has fallen into the hands of an artist it has been found worthy. Its low place in public esteem is due to no inherent defect, but only to the strange blindness of puppeteers and public alike to its tremendous possibilities.

# Plays for Younger Audiences

**A**lthough my earlier chapters have been concerned almost entirely with the presenting of plays for adult audiences, I have tried from time to time to suggest ways in which the excitement of the medium may be used to interest the young in types of serious drama with which they would not normally come into contact. The following specific suggestions may be useful to those who work in children's theatre and who are seeking material that may be exploited in this way.

Some types of drama must, of course, be eliminated from consideration entirely. Children enjoy movement, action, and color, and are easily bored by extended passages of dialogue. This means that Greek tragedy, for example, with its generally static on-stage action and its limited range of characters, is impossible. The best of Greek comedy, the work of Aristophanes, will also have to be avoided, partly, and obviously, on moral grounds and partly because his unique humor demands a degree of theatrical sophistication to which most children cannot attain. Selections would be possible. Much of the fantasy of *The Birds* would appeal to them, and Aristophanes' last play, *Wealth*, could be adapted without too much difficulty. This allegory of the blind god of wealth who has his sight restored and begins to distribute riches only to those who deserve them would be meaningful even to quite young audiences, particularly those who have done some reading in Greek mythology.

The later Greek comedy offers greater possibilities. The chief dramatist of the fourth century B.C. was Menander, a prolific playwright, most of whose work has unfortunately perished. Some plays, however, have survived in fragments, and in recent years a complete comedy has been discovered. This is the *Dyskolos*, easily available in a number of good translations under various titles—*The Grouch, The Misanthrope, The Bad-Tempered Man, The Man Who Didn't Like People*. It is basically a simple domestic comedy, involving an old farmer who hates his fellow men and refuses to have anything to do with neighbors or even his own family. A young man from Athens comes courting his daughter and is rudely rebuffed; there is a great deal of humorous comparison here between the soft life of the city and the rigors of the countryside. Then the old man falls down a well, and in his plight suffers a change of heart; he reflects that every man needs a friend at some point in his life, and is finally reconciled to those about him. Characterizations are simple, there is ample opportunity for interpolated comic business, and the play's appeal rests on several tried and proven comic formulas which will be understandable to any child who has ever watched television. Indeed, this play could form an admirable introduction to Greek theatre for audiences who would normally have no acquaintance with the field. Confronted with a play which is at the beginning of our own comic tradition, children will be surprised to find how little has changed in over two thousand years, and how, although the costumes have changed, the same jokes are still being made.

Roman comedy, the work of Plautus and Terence, will have to be avoided for the same reason as Aristophanes—they are broad and often obscene in their humor, and the plots usually spring from social situations which it takes maturity to comprehend. Some plays of Plautus could be adapted without too much loss. An obvious suggestion is the *Captivi* (*Prisoners of War*) which is more serious in tone than most of his work, and deals with a father's discovery that his long-lost son is working on his own estate as a slave. *Aulularia* (*The Pot of Gold*) could also be performed with minimal adaptation. Several of the other plays are possible, depending on the attitude of the teacher, the class, and the community.

Shakespeare offers a wealth of material. I have performed selections from various plays even to very young children with considerable success. One scene which has always proved popular is *The Tempest*, II 2. This is the episode where Caliban, unwillingly gathering wood for Prospero, meets the comic characters who have been shipwrecked in the recent storm—Trinculo the jester and Stephano the drunken butler. Caliban at first takes them for spirits, and they are equally intrigued by him. They then fall to drinking together, and the scene ends with songs and dances as the three make a plot to take over the island. There are several amusing pieces of business, particularly the moment when Trinculo, to escape the rain, crawls under Caliban's cloak as he lies prostrate on the ground, and is then taken by Stephano for a four-legged monster. This goes down very well with children, and presents little difficulty in manipulation.

Other single scenes can be excerpted from plays and given either as short classroom demonstrations or as items in a longer performance. In a different mood, the moving dialogue between Arthur and Hubert, *King John* IV 1, has several times been adapted to marionette performance. For those seeking something simpler than a whole play but of more sustained interest than a single scene, the sub-plot of *Twelfth Night* is almost ideal. These are the scenes showing the tricking of Malvolio and his supposed madness. They can be removed from their context and performed as an independent playlet which runs for about forty-five minutes. I have played such an adaptation constructed from the following scenes:

I 3. This is, strictly speaking, not relevant to the Malvolio episode, but serves to introduce the characters of Sir Toby, Sir Andrew, and Maria and give an idea of their conduct.

II 3. The drinking bout, interrupted by Malvolio, and the hatching of a plan of revenge.

II 5. The plan in action: the letter-reading scene.

III 3. Malvolio's appearance before Olivia in yellow stockings; the scene should end just before Sir Andrew's return with the challenge to the duel, which belongs to the main action.

IV 2. Malvolio imprisoned as a madman, and his persecution by the conspirators.

V 1. The scene begins with Olivia's "Fetch Malvolio hither," and ends with her "He hath been notoriously abused." The clown's song, "When that I was and a little tiny boy," can be used as a pendant to the playlet as it is to the complete play.

A few verbal changes will be needed, but not many, to make the scenes into a consistent whole. Relatively few characters are needed—Sir Toby Belch, Sir Andrew Ague-cheek, Maria, Malvolio, Feste the clown, Olivia, and the servant Fabian. This list can be further reduced by giving Fabian's part, as is often done in live productions, to Feste. The setting can be as elaborate or as simple as you please; I used a permanent set of three arches. Malvolio's prison cell was indicated by isolating him in a white spotlight on a stage lit dark blue overall. The only mechanical problem of any significance is the necessity of a costume change for Malvolio. I found it simpler, in single-handed operation, to construct two identical puppets, one with yellow stockings and one without; where there is more backstage help available this could be avoided.

In later comedy, a number of Molière's shorter farces

would make excellent material. These have the added advantage of being rarely done in any medium. Plays like *Monsieur de Porceaugnac* and *Le Médecin Malgré Lui* have enough violent action and buffoonery to keep the youngest audience entertained, and the stories are simple enough to be easily assimilable. The chief difficulty here would be in obtaining good acting versions, as adequate modern translations of the lesser-known Molière plays are hard to come by. Sheridan's *The Critic* could also be adapted into a short and amusing children's show. The first act, which is highly topical and full of references to the theatre of its own time, is of little interest now except to theatre historians, but the extended burlesque of the second act is splendidly funny still, whether one knows what Sheridan is burlesquing or not. I have given this part of *The Critic* using marionettes for the commentators, Puff, Sneer, and Dangle, and flat cardboard cutout figures of the Victorian "penny plain and tuppence colored" type for the characters of the play-within-the-play. My aim here was to indicate the pasteboard absurdity of the turgid historical drama that Sheridan was satirizing; but, of course, marionettes could be used equally well for both groups of characters.

# SELECTED BIBLIOGRAPHY

THE FOLLOWING are some of the more useful and important works in the field. All are easily accessible, and several contain their own more elaborate bibliographies.

## General

Beaumont, Cyril. *Puppets and Puppetry*. London: The Studio Ltd., New York: Studio Publications Inc., 1958. (Some of the material in this book first appeared in *Puppets and the Puppet Stage*, 1938.)

Bussell, Jan. *The Puppets and I*. London: Faber and Faber, 1950.

Obraztsov, Sergei. *My Profession*. Moscow: Foreign Languages Publishing House, 1950.

## Historical and Ethnic

Bowers, Faubion. *Japanese Theatre*. New York: Hill and Wang, 1959. (Contains two long sections on the Bunraku theatre and a translation of a Japanese puppet play.)

McPharlin, Paul. *The Puppet Theatre in America*. New York: Harper, 1949.

Magnin, Charles. *Histoire des marionettes en Europe depuis l'antiquité jusqu'à nos jours*. 2nd ed., Paris: Michel Levy Frères, 1862.

Martinovitch, Nicholas. *The Turkish Theatre*. New York: Theatre Arts Inc., 1933.

Obraztsov, Sergei. *The Chinese Puppet Theatre*. London: Faber and Faber, 1961.

Speaight, George. *The History of the English Puppet Theatre*. New York: De Graff, 1955.

### Technical

Batchelder, Marjorie. *The Puppet Theatre Handbook*. New York and London: Harper, 1947.

———. *Rod-Puppets and the Human Theatre*. Columbus: Ohio State University Press, 1947.

Beaton, Mabel and Les. *Marionettes: A Hobby for Everyone*. New York: Crowell, 1948.

Merton, George. *The Hand Puppets*. New York: Nelson, 1957.

———. *The Marionette*. New York: Nelson, 1957.

# INDEX

(Not all of the plays mentioned in this index are discussed in detail in the text. They are listed here principally to serve as an indication of the variety of source material available to the puppet theatre and may, thereby, aid in the selection of scripts.)